TIMEF⬤RM

HORSES TO

2019/20 JUMPS

GW00660289

CONTENTS

TIMEF0RM

ISBN 978-1-9997783-6-1   Price £10.95

Printed and bound by
Charlesworth Press,
Wakefield, UK 01924 204830

SECTION

Timeform's Fifty To Follow, carefully chosen by members of Timeform's editorial staff, are listed below with their respective page numbers. A selection of ten (**marked in bold with a ★**) is made for those who prefer a smaller list.

The form summary for each horse is shown after its age, colour, sex and pedigree. The summary shows the distance, the state of the going and where the horse finished in each of its races since the start of the 2017/18 season. Performances are in chronological sequence with the date of its last race shown at the end (F–ran on Flat).

The distance of each race is given in furlongs. Steeplechase form figures are prefixed by the letter 'c', hurdle form figures by the letter 'h' and NH Flat race or bumper form figures by the letter 'b'.

The going is symbolised as follows: f–firm, m–good to firm; g–good, d–good to soft; s–soft; v–heavy.

Placings are indicated, up to the sixth place, by use of superior figures, an asterisk being used to denote a win and superior letters are used to convey what happened to a horse during the race: F–fell, pu–pulled up, ur–unseated rider, bd–brought down, su–slipped up, ro–ran out.

The Timeform Rating of a horse is simply the merit of the horse expressed in pounds and is arrived at by careful examination of its running against other horses. The ratings range from 175+ for the champions down to a figure of around 55 for selling platers. Symbols attached to the ratings: 'p'–likely to improve; 'P'–capable of much better form; '+'–the horse may be better than we have rated it.

Ask Dillon (Ire) h129

6 b.g. Ask – Mum's Miracle (Ire) (Luso)
2018/19 b15.7g² b16d² b16.4g⁵ h21.6s* h18.5d² h21s h21.6s* Apr 16

Exciting times lie ahead for Fergal O'Brien and his upwardly mobile team. The former assistant to Nigel Twiston-Davies was quick to make his mark in the training ranks and, though just missing out on a third successive half century of winners in 2018/19, he looks ready to kick on again this season as he takes residence in his new state-of-the-art training base, Ravenswell Farm, located around 10 miles from Cheltenham racecourse. The early signs are promising with a flying start already made to the current campaign, and, in Ask Dillon, O'Brien has a novice chaser with the potential to make his mark in graded company.

A winning pointer for previous connections in Ireland, Ask Dillon showed fairly useful form without winning in three bumpers, before taking the switch to hurdles in his stride with a first success under Rules in an Ascot maiden last December, clearly relishing the step up to 21f on testing ground as he forged clear from the second last to win by seven lengths.

Being a son of Ask with a stout pedigree, it was already clear that staying would be Ask Dillon's forte, so it didn't come as a complete surprise when he was unable to defy a penalty when dropped back to 2¼m for an Exeter novice in February. Still, a staying-on second was another promising effort, and O'Brien had seen enough to pitch him in the Ballymore Novices' Hurdle

Ask Dillon offered plenty to work on over hurdles last season

at Cheltenham. That ultimately proved a step too far at this stage of his career, but it didn't take him long to bounce back, ending his hurdling season as he had begun with a ready success, this time by eight lengths in an ordinary 21f novice back at Exeter.

Ask Dillon has yet to race over 3m and beyond, but it's abundantly clear that that is where his future lies—with the size and scope to go with his undoubted staying ability, he looks a very useful staying novice chaser in the making. As for the O'Brien team, it's not only odds-on that they will better the 60 winners they achieved in 2017/18 in their new surroundings, but also that Ask Dillon will play his part in helping to realise that. Exciting times indeed. ***Fergal O'Brien***

Conclusion: *Good-topped gelding who enjoyed successful novice season over hurdles and looks ready to go up a notch or two in staying novice chases*

Baddesley Prince (Ire)   h116p

5 b.g. Doyen (Ire) – Norabella (Ire) (Shantou (USA))
2018/19 b15.7g⁵ h16.3d h16.7v h15.9d² h20.5dᶠ Mar 1

A tall, rather unfurnished gelding, Baddesley Prince is certainly bred to make his mark over jumps—he is out of an unraced half-sister to the useful hurdler/smart chaser (2¾m-4m winner) Back In Focus, who in turn was out of the smart 2½m chase winner Dun Belle—and there was enough promise in his debut campaign over hurdles to suggest that Chris Gordon is likely to be winning races with him sooner rather than later.

It was probably his pedigree that saw Baddesley Prince sent off at just 2/1 for his debut in a weak-looking newcomers' bumper at Southwell last September, but he ultimately failed to make an impact, finding himself outpaced leaving the back straight and unable to get on terms with the principals. He didn't fare much better on his first two starts over hurdles, either, beaten a combined 43 lengths in novices at Newbury and Bangor, though he did hint at ability on both occasions under considerate handling, leaving the impression that he was being brought along with handicaps in mind.

Baddesley Prince then showed much more than he had previously when second on his final qualifying run at Plumpton, finding only a thriving sort who had some solid form at the track too strong. He was doing all his best work at the finish, too—hardly surprising given the stamina on the dam's side of the pedigree—strongly suggesting that he may yet have even more to offer when going beyond 2m.

Unfortunately for his connections, Baddesley Prince didn't get the chance to show as much when making his handicap debut over 2½m at Newbury in March—he fell at the fourth—but the overwhelming feeling remains that we are only just scratching the surface of his potential. With his novice status still intact, it will be interesting to see which way connections go with him this term, but handicaps still appeal as the environment in which he will be seen to maximum effect, with a BHA mark of 115 highly unlikely to prove his limit. *Chris Gordon*

Conclusion: *Unexposed hurdler who looks generously handicapped and is one to keep on the right side in races beyond 2m*

 ## Bako de La Saulaie (Fr)   c122
8 b.g. Balko (Fr) – Krickette (Fr) (Passing Sale (Fr))
2018/19 c20.1s³ c26.2g² c24.2s² Dec 8

'Season 2018/19 has been one to forget for everyone at Hazelrigg and, to be honest, I was glad to see the back of it a few weeks ago at Sandown.'

Writing a blog post on her website entitled 'Unwanted summer break' in May, Rose Dobbin summed up the difficulties faced by her string last season better than we ever could, with the bugs that plagued the yard throughout resulting in her saddling only seven winners, well down on the personal-best tally of 25 that she recorded during the previous campaign. So desperate did the situation become that Dobbin took the decision to take all her horses out of training at the time of the aforementioned blog post, and, with the new campaign fast approaching, you have to go back to the Perth meeting on April 26th to find the last runners that she saddled, all of which finished well beaten.

The trainer issued a far more positive bulletin about the health of her string when they returned from the paddocks in July, though, and there's a fair chance that she has some well-handicapped horses at her disposal if things stay that way in the coming months, with Bako de La Saulaie appealing as one to look out for when resuming over fences from a BHA mark of 125.

Admittedly, he has proved rather expensive to follow in seven chase starts to date, but there was plenty of encouragement to be taken from his truncated 2018/19 campaign, when he impressed with his consistency by being placed in all three starts. The career-best effort he produced when beaten just three quarters of a length on the final occasion in a 3m novices' handicap at Wetherby suggests that he is still on an upward curve over fences, and, given plenty of time to recover from what was ailing him and his stablemates subsequently, it will be disappointing if he can't shed his maiden tag over fences before progressing through the handicap ranks. He has raced mainly on ground softer than good. *Rose Dobbin*

Conclusion: *Remains a maiden after seven starts over fences, but nothing wrong with his attitude; well up to winning races from his current mark provided that his yard is firing on all cylinders after a barren summer*

Bourbon Borderline (Ire)   b96p

5 b.g. Milan – Daraheen Diamond (Ire) (Husyan (USA))
2018/19 b16d³ Mar 28

A €57,000 purchase as a three-year-old, Bourbon Borderline fell before the race could take shape on his point debut at Boulta last December, but, clearly none the worse for that, he then took apart inferior opposition in a maiden at Dromahane just a fortnight later. A transfer out of Colin Bowe's yard ensued, and he was all the rage in the ring ahead of his bumper debut for Dan Skelton at Warwick three months later (fitted with a tongue strap). A wide course on that occasion didn't help Bourbon Borderline's cause, and having loomed up menacingly on the turn, he ultimately found an experienced opponent in Welsh Saint too streetwise, losing second close home for good measure. The form of that bumper has yet to be fully tested, but the vibes are that it's an above-average contest, and it may be significant that Skelton has seemingly targeted that race in the past, winning it three times in all, notably with Whiskey In The Jar to continue the transatlantic-liquor theme.

On both looks and pedigree, Bourbon Borderline is a promising sort, possessing the physique of a chaser and a name very much in keeping with the boozy connection in his family; he's a brother to Brewin'upastorm, who quickly developed into a useful novice hurdler last season, signing off with a good second in the Mersey Novices' Hurdle at Aintree. Connections will presumably switch straight to obstacles this season, a task he should be more than up to, and it would come as no surprise were he to attain a useful level of form over hurdles. *Dan Skelton*

Conclusion: *Shaped well in a warm-looking bumper on Rules debut and is fancied to emulate brother Brewin'upastorm by ending up useful over obstacles himself this term*

Follow us on Twitter @Timeform

Bright Forecast (Ire) ★   h146p

5 b.g. Arcadio (Ger) – Check The Forecast (Ire) (Shernazar)
2018/19 h16.3s* h15.5g* h15.7d² h21s³ Mar 13

'He appears to be a natural over a fence. Exciting times ahead.' Ben Pauling's ringing endorsement of Bright Forecast is something to warm the hearts of National Hunt enthusiasts as the winter months draw in. How high the five-year-old can go is open to question, but there's little doubting that in the short term he promises to take very high rank among the staying novice chasers if Pauling's assertion holds true. And after that, well who knows? But the Cheltenham Gold Cup is certainly not out of the equation in the years to come if all things run smoothly and well.

Pauling, however, knows better than most the highs and lows of jumps racing, having tragically lost his flag bearer Willoughby Court so prematurely last season. And Bright Forecast also holds the distinction of being the last horse owner Nick Embiricos was involved in before his sad passing last November. The name Embiricos might not immediately strike a chord with all racing fans, but his famous white and blue silks were etched into racing folklore when Aldaniti claimed the most amazing of Grand National wins back in 1981. Now Pauling and owners the Aldaniti partnership have another potential star in the making on their hands.

Bright Forecast ran only four times over hurdles in 2018/19, but he already rates as very smart after posting an excellent staying-on third behind City Island and Champ in the 21f Ballymore Novices' Hurdle at Cheltenham on the last of those starts. He still looked far from the finished article there, too, getting tapped for foot from two out before fairly storming up the hill and hinting strongly that a step up to 3m+ would see him to even better effect.

That was Bright Forecast's first race beyond 2m and it clearly suited him well, but he'd already hinted that much better things were on the horizon when overcoming distinct greenness to land a hot Newbury maiden on his debut. A bloodless Leicester novice win followed before he gave fellow *Fifty* member Mister Fisher a real fright in a Grade 2 event at Haydock.

Expect Bright Forecast to win plenty of novice chases and be back at Cheltenham in March as a serious candidate for the RSA Chase. **Ben Pauling**

Conclusion: *Exciting novice hurdler last season with the scope and potential to take very high rank in the staying novice chase division*

Captain Moirette (Fr) ★   h128

7 gr.g. Kap Rock (Fr) – Rahana Moirette (Fr) (Dom Alco (Fr))
2018/19 h16d⁴ h15.7m* h15.7d* h16m Apr 13

Captain Moirette wasn't an expensive purchase by modern-day standards, costing only £10,000 as a three-year-old, but even that was starting to look money down the drain by the time that the 2018/19 campaign came around. Indeed, having displayed plenty of ability in three bumpers in early-2016—while bringing in very little in the way of a return on his connections' investment—it was then another 1000 days before he was seen on a racecourse again due to injury.

Plenty has happened in the last 12 months, however, and Captain Moirette now has the look of a very shrewd buy having rapidly made up for lost time since returning at Wetherby last December. Making his hurdling debut on that occasion, he again showcased plenty of ability under a cold ride, smoothly getting into contention by the home turn before excusably tiring after a mistake two out, ultimately beaten nearly eight lengths into fourth. Wisely given plenty of time to recover from that effort, he then showed much-improved form to get off the mark in a novice hurdle that has worked out well at Catterick in February, before taking another step forward to follow up under a penalty at Haydock the following month. There was a marked improvement in his jumping on that occasion, typically travelling strongly before drawing clear approaching the last flight and winning with more in hand than the five-length winning margin would suggest.

Captain Moirette wasn't up to the task when stepped up markedly in grade for the Scottish Champion Hurdle at Ayr on his final start, but that performance shouldn't detract from his long-term potential, with a switch to fences likely to be in the offing this season. Every inch a chaser on looks, his connections are likely to have had that career in mind ever since parting with their cash for him back in 2015, and while the road here may not have been entirely smooth, it would be a surprise if Captain Moirette didn't have his best days still ahead of him. He has raced exclusively at 2m to date but should be suited by further. *Sue Smith*

Conclusion: *Big, scopey sort who had a good first season over obstacles and should be at least as effective when going over fences in the coming months*

Dan Barber (**Captain Moirette**): *"It might not be at the level of 'Sir Michael Stoute's horses tend to improve with age', or even 'you've got to get up the hill at Cheltenham', in the long list of racing truisms, but the notion that Sue Smith's horses tend to flourish over fences more than hurdles does indeed warrant full attention, even more so when the animal in question is built like Captain Moirette, a grey as rangy as he is striking who did extremely well in a light first campaign over the smaller obstacles. Yes, the Scottish Champion Hurdle proved a bridge too far on his final outing, but Captain Moirette had already proven himself a fairly useful novice in winning his previous two outings, despite having endured a mammoth 1000-day absence following a spell in bumpers in 2015/16. He can further make up for lost time this season."*

Cilaos Glace (Fr)   h123p

6 br.g. Voix du Nord (Fr) – Miss Glacee (Fr) (Mister Mat (Fr))
2018/19 h16s[4] h16d h19.6d[6] h17.7v* h16d* Apr 6

The 'anything he achieves over hurdles is a bonus' adage is overused in racing, but it's surely long odds-on that Cilaos Glace improves on his timber form immediately over the larger obstacles, especially if returning in the same rich vein of form as when winning the final two starts of his novice campaign over hurdles. He reaped the benefit of considerate rides early in his career when running out a 33-length winner of a weak maiden in heavy ground at Fontwell in March, before defying an opening mark of 118 to follow up in a big-field handicap at Chepstow a month later, quickly putting his seal on the race early in the straight.

His pedigree screams chaser given that his dam, Miss Glacee, won over fences and is a half-sister to Ice Mood, a Grade 1 winner over the larger obstacles in France. His sire Voix du Nord is also in vogue as the sire of Kemboy, Espoir d'Allen and Vroum Vroum Mag, to name but three. When you also factor in that he's a well-made gelding who has an exuberant way of going about things, Cilaos Glace surely possesses the scope to excel over fences. Whether connections elect to tackle a maiden/novice or pitch him straight into handicap company remains to be seen, but, either way, he is a six-year-old to keep on the right side of; it would come as no surprise were he to end up in a high-end handicap at one of the spring festivals at around 2m–2¼m. *Oliver Sherwood*

Conclusion: *Ended last season on the up over hurdles and has the looks, pedigree and demeanour to suggest that he can only improve for the switch to fences*

Cloth Cap (Ire)   c135p

7 b.g. Beneficial – Cloth Fair (Ire) (Old Vic)
2018/19 c19.9g[3] c22.6g* c25.2g* c31.8m[3] Apr 13

Next year's Grand National will mark the 15-year anniversary of Trevor Hemmings' first win in the race with Hedgehunter, who has since been joined on the roll of honour by Ballabriggs (2011) and Many Clouds (2015) to secure the Lancashire businessman's place amongst the most successful owners in the history of the Aintree showpiece.

Overall, Hemmings has been represented in every renewal since 2000, though he has often been forced to reach for his cheque book to maintain that record, with some last-minute purchases paying off more than others—Vicente, for example, fell at the first in the 2017 Grand National having been bought for the task just a month earlier, before belatedly rewarding his new owner's investment with a second successive win in the Scottish equivalent later in April.

Hemmings is likely to be spared the task of scouring the transfer market in 2020, with Cloth Cap—who shares his name with an item of clothing almost as synonymous with his owner as the Grand National—already appearing to possess all the right attributes for Aintree, a sound jumper who may yet have even more to offer after only four starts over fences.

A useful hurdler in 2017/18, it didn't take Cloth Cap long to prove himself a better chaser last term, quickly stepping up on his debut third with back-to-back wins in handicaps at Stratford and Catterick. However, it was his final start in the Scottish Grand National that really identified him as one to keep on the right on the side of this season; one of only four sent off at single-figure odds in a field of 23, he showed much-improved form on his first try at marathon trips, holding every chance entering the straight and keeping on well thereafter to be beaten only four lengths into third behind Takingrisks.

Still only a seven-year-old, Cloth Cap's lack of experience makes the way that he handled himself at Ayr even more impressive, looking a natural in the heat of one of the most competitive handicaps of the entire National Hunt season. A BHA mark of 137 certainly looks workable on that evidence (he'd almost certainly need a rise in the weights to make the cut at Aintree), and with further improvement on the cards, he is one to be positive about in staying handicaps en route to the Grand National. Cloth Cap won on soft ground over hurdles, but his run at Ayr showed that he acts well under firmer conditions. *Jonjo O'Neill*

Conclusion: *Progressive sort who has age on his side and looks likely to be a fixture in the big staying handicaps this season; potentially overpriced for the Grand National at 66/1*

Copperhead   h123p

5 ch.g. Sulamani (Ire) – How's Business (Josr Algarhoud (Ire))
2018/19 h16.3d h19.7s³ h20.5s h18.5s* h19.8s* Feb 15

Having just read Copperhead by Alexi Zentner, a hard-hitting novel depicting a sinister side to small-town America (described as *'one of the bravest, most bracing novels I've read in years'* by The New York book review), I was struck by the sheer luck of one's family and how big a part factors beyond your own control can mould you. Fortunately, the equine Copperhead is in the care of Colin Tizzard, so could hardly be in better hands to flourish on the racecourse.

Copperhead failed to trouble the judge in his first three starts in novice hurdles last season, but that had more to do with the depth of the races he contested, rather than any attempt by his conditions to hide his light under a bushel. An opening BHA mark of 104 failed to reflect that fact as he took apart seven rivals at Exeter in January, while a bad error two out looked to scupper his follow-up attempt at Sandown a month later, but he overcame that blunder to ultimately score by four lengths, indicative of one comfortably ahead of his mark.

Connections may attempt to complete a hat-trick over hurdles upon his return to action, but, given the physique Copperhead possesses, it's surely only a matter of time before he is switched to fences (dam How's Business was a big mare who achieved useful form over both hurdles and fences). There is certainly no finer man to prepare him for that transition than Tizzard, for whom any number of horses have blossomed when going chasing—fellow *Fifty* member Mister Malarky is a case in point, given that he was Timeform-rated 116 after his first season over hurdles but ended last term rated 149 over fences with us. Copperhead starts from a higher base following his two hurdling wins, and with longer trips still to explore (yet to race beyond 2½m), it wouldn't be remiss to speculate that he could be a Timeform 140+ horse by the end of the season, too. ***Colin Tizzard***

Conclusion: *Ended last season on the up with a brace of handicap wins over hurdles and looks to have every chance of climbing higher still if making the switch to chasing this term; likely to stay 3m*

Deyrann de Carjac (Fr)   c133p
6 b.g. Balko (Fr) – Queyrann (Fr) (Sheyrann)
2018/19 h16g* h16d² h16.4gF h19.6d² h18.6d² h16m⁵ :: 2019/20 c21.2v* May 29

It's fair to say that Cartmel is something of an anomaly as far as National Hunt tracks go, with all the venue's nine meetings taking place between May and August. Given that most of Britain's leading jumpers are already enjoying their first taste of summer grass by the time the action in Cumbria gets underway, it stands to reason that the standard of racing leaves a bit to be desired, but there is still no end of entertainment to be enjoyed—the idiosyncratic track sees to that—and there are invariably a few gems to be unearthed, with Deyrann de Carjac, in particular, appealing as one to follow on the evidence of his successful chase debut at the course in May.

Deyrann de Carjac showed himself to be capable of fairly useful form over hurdles in 2018/19, easily winning his first start of the campaign, a maiden against limited opposition at Warwick last May, before returning from five months off the track with a good second in a novice at Chepstow, when beaten only two lengths under a penalty by fellow *Fifty* member Pym. Admittedly, Deyrann de Carjac failed to get his head in front again in four subsequent outings over the smaller obstacles that season, but he did show comparable form in defeat on a couple of occasions, and, given his physique (has plenty of scope), it was always likely to be when switching to fences that he came into his own.

That certainly proved to be the case when making a successful start to his chasing career at Cartmel, looking a good prospect as he drew clear after the last, winning by 13 lengths from a pair who were rated higher than him over hurdles. It was always the plan to give him a break after that according to trainer Alan King, who is hopeful that he can make up into a '*pretty decent*' novice chaser this season; he is already useful on the Timeform scale, and with further progress on the cards, it will be disappointing if there aren't more races to be won with him through the winter months (the going was unseasonably heavy at Cartmel). ***Alan King***

Conclusion: *Created a good impression on his debut over fences and should continue to do well in novice chases around 2m–2½m; BHA mark of 137 also looks workable*

Dorking Cock (Ire) h120

5 b.g. Winged Love (Ire) – Kiss Jolie (Fr) (Cadoudal (Fr))
2018/19 h19.2s³ h20g h15.7s h19.7s³ h16s* h17g* h17v² Mar 17

The *'Dorking'* was a breed of cockerel bred by the Romans for its meat and has since developed into the symbol of Dorking town (a three-metre high cockerel statue sits on the Deepdene Roundabout). It's reported that the breed topped its class in the Zoological Society's first poultry show in 1845, and, in the much the same vein, it will be disappointing if the equine Dorking Cock isn't competing for a few prizes himself if going over fences this season.

Well held in his first three starts in novice hurdles in 2018/19, Dorking Cock took a significant step forward when third on his handicap debut in what turned out to be a pretty warm race at Wetherby (2½m) on Boxing Day, likely to have finished closer than the six and a quarter lengths he was beaten, too, but for an error at the second last. He duly did his bit for the form of that race when dropped back to 2m for his next start at Sandown in February, leading on the bridle approaching two out and quickly forging clear thereafter, winning by six lengths with plenty in hand.

Wisely turned out only three days later from the same mark, Dorking Cock was inevitably all the rage to follow up at Carlisle (17f), and though he briefly looked in trouble, he again showed a willing attitude to prevail by a length and a half from one who won next-time-out. A narrow defeat for Dorking Cock in a four-runner race back at Carlisle a month later was no disgrace, either, running at least as well in defeat (from 9 lb higher) as when recording both his wins.

It's unclear whether Dorking Cock will make the immediate switch to the larger obstacles this season, but he's a good-topped gelding who promises to excel over fences, with a return to 2½m also sure to suit; a current BHA mark of 122 should prove well within his compass. *Tom Lacey*

Conclusion: *Progressed well over hurdles last season and should prove capable of better still this term, with a switch to novice handicap company over fences a potentially fruitful route to take*

Ena Baie (Fr) h124p

5 b.m. Crillon (Fr) – Trema Baie (Fr) (Snow Cap (Fr))
2018/19 h15.7d⁴ :: 2019/20 h15.8d² h15.7d* h16.5g⁴ Jul 31

Ena Baie was purchased privately by J. P. McManus following her victory in a bumper when trained in France by Yannick Fertillet. She had done well to win on that occasion, finishing strongly from the back of the field to score by a length, and, as a result, big things were clearly expected of her when she made her British debut in a similar event at Cheltenham in January 2018.

Ultimately, fourth was the best that Ena Baie could manage that day, though she shaped much better than the bare result, with the much softer ground than she had previously encountered possibly against her. The fact that she was off the track for 11 months subsequently suggests that she may have been amiss, too, and her belated reappearance at Southwell—when fourth on her hurdling debut after a wind operation—proved a fleeting one, with racegoers having to wait another seven months after that before we saw her again.

She then offered something to work on when second at Ffos Las in June, finding only a progressive sort with race fitness on her side too strong, before building on that with a first success on these shores on her handicap debut back at Southwell later that month. The bare form was nothing special from a BHA mark of just 108, but she was value for extra on the day, and it didn't take her long to confirm herself a mare on the up, improving again when fourth in a 20-runner handicap at Galway on her final start, still nearer last than first two furlongs from home, before staying on strongly after the last to snatch a minor placing on the line.

A lightly-raced mare, who has worn a hood on her last three starts, Ena Baie has certainly shown enough to suggest that she is up to winning more races from her current mark, with the prospect of even more to come, and it would be no surprise if she proved capable of racking up a sequence before contesting some of the top-end races in the spring. *Harry Fry*

Conclusion: *Unexposed mare who is up to winning more races over hurdles from what is still a lenient mark*

 ## Espoir de Guye (Fr)   h116

5 b.g. Khalkevi (Ire) – Penelope de Guye (Fr) (Dom Alco (Fr))
2018/19 h17.9s⁵ h18.9g* h19.7s h16s² Mar 10

Venetia Williams has historically done well with her French recruits, and Espoir de Guye looks another promising purchase having shaped well on his debut over hurdles in his native France, before winning a four-year-old event at Les Sables-d'Olonne, beating a next-time-out winner by a length.

Purchased by new connections for €70,000 at the sales in July 2018, he proved very easy to back ahead of his British debut in a novice hurdle at Hereford four months later and duly shaped as if badly in need of the run. Espoir de Guye then wasn't seen for another three months, during which time he underwent a breathing operation, which seemed to work the oracle as he returned to the sort of form that he had produced in France when finishing runner-up in a novice at Warwick on his final start. That run came back at 2m, and he firmly left the impression that he would be much happier back over further, outpaced in the leader's slipstream entering the straight but sticking to the task well.

Williams has often targeted that race in recent years—she won back-to-back renewals with Belami des Pictons (2016) and Grand Turina (2017), while Cloudy Glen was also second in 2018—and Espoir de Guye appeals as very much the type to go on from that and take his form up a notch this season. The handicapper has given him a mark of 120, which is more than fair based on his French form, and it is surely only a matter of time before he opens his account on these shores if standing more regular racing, with 2½m likely to prove his optimum trip. **Venetia Williams**

Conclusion: *Compact gelding who shaped well on his final start and is one to follow in low-level handicaps from what looks a workable opening mark*

 # Fanfan du Seuil (Fr)   h129

4 b.g. Racinger (Fr) – Nina du Seuil (Fr) (Blushing Flame (USA))
2018/19 h16dF h16.8s* h16.8d² h16.4s⁵ h17d Apr 4

Each year more and more horses with '*du Seuil*' in their name are appearing on British shores, with Defi du Seuil—an unbeaten juvenile hurdler in 2016/17 who has since developed into a high-class chaser—perhaps the best known of them all. It's fair to say that Fanfan du Seuil didn't reach quite the same heights in his own juvenile campaign last season, but he still showcased plenty of ability on occasions and strikes as very much the type to do even better this term.

A good-topped gelding, Fanfan du Seuil won a three-year-old hurdle on his sole start in France and was well backed for his British debut in a juvenile event at Chepstow last October, where he was in the process of shaping well when falling two out, keeping on in third and yet to be asked for maximum effort at the time. That experience clearly wasn't lost on him when lining up at Exeter the following month, as he confirmed all and more of the promise shown previously to beat a next-time-out winner by five lengths, readily asserting on the run-in.

Fanfan du Seuil also went like the best horse at the weights on his next start in a useful event on Cheltenham Trials Day, nursed to the front after the last before idling and getting overhauled in the final 50 yards, a very strong headwind perhaps not helping matters. The handicapper gave him an opening mark of 136 on the back of that performance, which looked lenient on the face of it, and Fanfan du Seuil went a long way to proving as much when fifth in the Fred Winter at the Cheltenham Festival, where he was unlucky not to finish closer having been hampered briefly and forced to switch approaching the last.

It would be unfair to judge him too harshly on his well-held seventh in Grade 1 company at Aintree on his final start, with the distance he was beaten possibly exaggerated by the big forward move he made entering the straight (tired late on). Previous remarks about him being potentially well treated are still very much valid, and, given how well suited he looked to the big-field scenario of the Fred Winter, it would be no surprise if his connections are eyeing up some of the season's major handicap hurdles at around 2m, with further improvement on the cards. **Tom George**

Conclusion: *Lightly-raced type who should have more to offer in handicaps from a BHA mark of 136*

Geordie B   h131p

6 gr.g. Geordieland (Fr) – Sari Rose (Fr) (Vertical Speed (Fr))
2018/19 h19.3g⁶ h19.7s² h23s* h23.1s* Mar 18

Venetia Williams has become synonymous with staying chasers in recent years, with Houblon des Obeaux, Katenko, Tenor Nivernais and 2009 Grand National winner Mon Mome featuring amongst those to have represented her with distinction in some of the bigger staying handicaps this century. It's fair to say that they give Geordie B some big shoes to fill, but he is very much in the mould of a future staying chaser, having showcased a massive engine on numerous occasions during his short career to date.

It was encouraging that Geordie B made a winning debut in a bumper at Hereford given that he is bred to stay so well over jumps—he is out of a half-sister to the very smart chaser (stayed 29f) Indien Bleu—and, for all that that race didn't work out, his subsequent form over hurdles marks him down as an exciting staying prospect. Admittedly, his hurdling career didn't start so well—he was well held under less-testing conditions than previously on his hurdling debut over 2½m at Ascot last November—but a return to soft ground over the same trip at Hereford the following month saw him much more in his comfort zone, leaving his debut form well behind as he went down by just a short head at the hands of the penalised winner.

It was when Geordie B was stepped up to 3m that he really found his feet, though, looking a thorough stayer as he opened his account in a novice at Lingfield (by four lengths from a next-time-out winner) in January. He then followed up under a penalty in a similar event at Exeter 11 weeks later, doing so in authoritative fashion, too, hitting the front on the approach to the last and always in control thereafter, winning by seven lengths with a bit in hand.

Geordie B remains with potential over hurdles if connections choose to stay in this sphere, though his long-term future almost certainly lies in long-distance chases, having left the impression in both of his wins last season that he still had plenty left in the tank.
Venetia Williams

Conclusion: *Rather unfurnished gelding who remains open to improvement when the emphasis is on stamina (will be suited by 3m+), with a switch to fences likely to be the making of him, too*

Get In The Queue ★   b119

5 b.g. Mount Nelson – Amarullah (Fr) (Daylami (Ire))
2018/19 b15.8s* b16.8d* b16.3d* Mar 23

Unlike the majority of sports, where those at the twilight of their careers tend to bow out quietly, it has become commonplace in racing that a retiring jockey does their level best to go out on a winner. Very few have the luxury of enjoying the armchair ride that Noel Fehily did, though, with the veteran pilot being able to call upon the exciting Get In The

Queue for his swansong in the Goffs UK Spring Sales Bumper at Newbury in March. Indeed, the *'fairytale'* ending was never really in doubt given that Get In The Queue was a 3/1-on shot, courtesy of two earlier wins by a combined 25 lengths, overcoming greenness on his debut at Uttoxeter in December, before posting a Timeform rating of 119 when routing the opposition in the fog at Exeter two months later, a figure surpassed by only three bumper horses in Britain and Ireland last season (the first three home in the Champion Bumper).

At this stage, it's fairly easy to draw comparisons with If The Cap Fits, given that he was a smart bumper performer for the same connections back in 2016/17. He was also prominent in the betting for the following season's Supreme Novices' Hurdle after creating an excellent impression in winning his first three starts in novice hurdles, and, though he was ultimately ruled out of Cheltenham through injury, that has not stopped him developing into a very smart performer at up to 3m, most recently showing a superb attitude to land the Liverpool Hurdle at Aintree in April.

It's hard to know what Get In The Queue's optimum trip will be—he certainly shapes as though he'll stay further than 2m, but his Flat pedigree (by Mount Nelson and out of a Daylami mare) offers hope for those looking to take the 33/1 currently on offer for the Supreme. The fact that he's been kept away from graded company up to now may partially explain why he is such a big price, but he still achieved plenty in the relatively calm waters that he was mixing in, rated higher than If The Cap Fits at the same stage of his career, and it is not hard to see him taking high rank amongst this season's crop of novice hurdlers. **Harry Fry**

Conclusion: *Made faultless start to his career, winning a trio of bumpers by an aggregate of nearly 30 lengths, and looks to have all the necessary tools to make up into a smart novice hurdler; will stay 2½m but clearly not short of speed*

Getariver (Ire)   b102+
6 br.m. Getaway (Ger) – Watson River (Ire) (Presenting)
2018/19 b14g* b16.3d* Mar 1

A £30,000 purchase after winning her sole start in Irish points, Getariver showed fairly useful form when winning both her starts in bumpers last season, and, as long as her energies can be channelled correctly (has tendency to take a strong hold), she looks as good a prospect as we've seen on this side of the Irish Sea for novice hurdles against her own sex.

Sent off 4/1 for her Rules debut at Ludlow in January, she created a favourable impression in beating the boys by eight lengths, taking a keen hold before being asked for her effort two furlongs out and quickening decisively clear of a next-time-out winner. She then followed up under a penalty at Newbury 43 days later, deserving extra credit, too, as she was once again too exuberant during the race, going to the front before halfway and clear of the remainder five furlongs from home, but displaying a good attitude to hold on in the closing stages.

Both her pedigree and demeanour suggest that she will be well suited by the switch to jumping, while there are mixed messages in terms of trip—there is plenty of stamina on the dam's side of her pedigree, so she should be suited by further than 2m in theory, though, given how free she was in her two bumper starts, sticking to the minimum trip is possibly the way to go in the short term.

In any case, she should be well up to winning a novice hurdle before having her sights raised, with the Dawn Run at the Cheltenham Festival appealing as an obvious end-of-season target. *Dan Skelton*

Conclusion: *Rather unfurnished mare who is unbeaten in a point and two bumpers, identifying herself as one to follow in novice hurdles against her own sex*

Getaway Trump (Ire) ★   h153p

6 b.g. Getaway (Ger) – Acinorev (Ire) (Cape Cross (Ire))

2018/19 h19.5g⁴ h20.5g* h16.8s* h20.5d² h15.7d⁴ h18.1d⁴ h16m* h16g* Apr 27

Paul Nicholls has seen most things in racing, but even he confessed to being surprised by the amount of progress shown last season by Getaway Trump, who failed to win in two bumper starts in 2017/18, but quickly proved a different proposition when switching to hurdles.

Getaway Trump jumps the last on his way to victory at Sandown

A promising fourth on his debut at Chepstow was quickly followed by easy novice wins at Plumpton and Exeter, setting up him up perfectly for a crack at the Challow Hurdle at Newbury, where he improved again in going down by only two and a half lengths at the hands of Champ, having cruised into contention. An excellent fourth when pitched into open handicap company in Ascot's Betfair Hurdle came next, shaping better than the bare result on the day, too, having been forced to deliver his challenge from further back than ideal. That effort was off a BHA rating of 142, and, by our reckoning, he had already improved to the tune of 49 lb since his Chepstow introduction.

His only modest run followed when an odds-on fourth back in novice company at Kelso, but it's worth noting that stablemate Black Corton also disappointed on that card, and Nicholls is of the opinion that they suffered a poor journey up to the Scottish track. Whatever ailed him there, he was right back on his game when returned to Scotland to Ayr for a qualifier for Sandown's Novices' Championship Final in April, easily scooting six lengths clear. That left him on an official mark of 147 and top weight of 11st 12lb for a seemingly competitive handicap at the Esher track. But Getaway Trump had saved his best until last and cruised round on the heels of the leaders until sent on approaching the second last, keeping on strongly under minimal pressure from Harry Cobden for an impressive two and three quarter length defeat of fellow *Fifty* member Harambe.

A winning pointer, Getaway Trump is a real chasing type, and while a campaign geared around the Champion Hurdle had been considered, Nicholls has ultimately taken the decision to change course, with a novice campaign over fences planned for 2019/20. Getaway Trump stays 21f but there is no doubt that speed is his primary asset, and, all being well, there is no reason why he shouldn't make up into a serious contender for the Arkle at the Cheltenham Festival. *Paul Nicholls*

Conclusion: *Progressed at a rate of knots in novice campaign over hurdles and rates a most exciting prospect now embarking on a chasing career; quotes of around 16/1 for the Arkle make plenty of appeal*

Phil Turner(Getaway Trump): *"There is no 'fake news' about the fact Getaway Trump is one of the most exciting novice chase prospects for 2019/20. It might have taken him until the final day of last season to show his full potential over hurdles, when defying top weight in a valuable novice handicap at Sandown, but he'd long shaped as if he had a lofty rating in him and is clearly a Grade 1 performer in the making. Getaway Trump is built to be a chaser and, in common with most from the Paul Nicholls yard, promises to do even better over the larger obstacles."*

Glen Rocco
c140p

8 ch.g. Shirocco (Ger) – Adees Dancer (Danehill Dancer (Ire))
2018/19 c16s^{ur} c21.6d* c20s^3 c20.5g^2 c24g* c24g^6 Feb 23

Owners and punters alike often curse their luck when '*bumping into one*', and the ownership group connected with Glen Rocco—including TV host Jeremy Kyle—had every reason to feel disconsolate when he found only Glen Forsa too strong at Kempton on Boxing Day. Of course, that rival was sent off 9/2 to win the Arkle three months later (ironically let down by his jumping, which was a major asset prior to that race), so it wasn't a major surprise that Glen Rocco did his bit for the form of that contest when defying a 3 lb higher mark back at that venue next time, seemingly relishing the step up to 3m as he annihilated the opposition by 23 lengths. His sixth over the same C&D in February may lead one or two to suggest that he's now summed up by his mark, but that would surely be a mistake given that he was unsuited by how the race developed, while the fourth and fifth both winning emphatically next time confirms that the beaten horses that day remain of interest. It should also be pointed out that Glen Rocco, a winning pointer, has had only eight career starts under Rules, so there's every chance that he may have more to offer as a second-season chaser, one who is likely to find a good handicap pot over 3m+ coming his way during the winter months (acts on soft going). ***Nick Gifford***

Conclusion: *Stout stayer who can boast strong form at Kempton last winter and has an unexposed profile that marks him out as one to keep onside in high-end handicaps over 3m+*

Grand Mogul (Ire)
b99p

5 br.g. Presenting – Oligarch Society (Ire) (Moscow Society (USA))
2018/19 b16g* Dec 22

It's tough to know whether Grand Mogul is named after a Donald Duck character, a peak in Idaho or neither given the nod to Russian influence on the dam-side of his pedigree, but, whatever its origin, the name Grand Mogul is one that we could be hearing a lot more of as he embarks on a campaign in novice hurdles this season.

Grand Mogul really caught the eye when fourth on his debut for Gordon Elliott in a big-field bumper at Punchestown in April 2018, doing well to finish as close as he did after being hampered by a faller on the home turn, with a pair of next-time-out winners immediately in front of him at the line. It was another eight months before we saw him again, but he had little trouble opening his own account when eventually reappearing in an ordinary contest at Thurles, well on the top at the finish despite still showing signs of inexperience during the race (went in snatches).

A transfer from Elliott rarely results in an upturn in fortunes, but he's joined another top-notch trainer in Nicky Henderson. On breeding, Grand Mogul will surely improve for the switch to obstacles and a greater test of stamina—he is by Presenting and out of a half-sister to Irish Grand National winner Thunder And Roses, while his brother Brahma Bull opened his hurdling account at the first time of asking over 3m.

Both that and how strong he was at the finish on debut suggest that he's likely to begin his novice campaign over further than 2m, and it would be no surprise to see him hit the ground running for his new yard, with Nicky Henderson-trained inmates rarely found wanting for know-how when starting out in this discipline. **Nicky Henderson**

Conclusion: *Confirmed promise of Rules debut (strong form) with ready win at Thurles last December; joined another top yard in the interim and looks a good prospect for novice hurdles over 2½m+*

Greaneteen (Fr) h128p

5 b.g. Great Pretender (Ire) – Manson Teene (Fr) (Mansonnien (Fr))
2018/19 h16v⁶ h18.5d* h17.7s* Jan 27

A half-brother to a couple of useful hurdlers in France, Greaneteen was purchased by his current connections for €145,000 after finishing third in a newcomers' hurdle at Clairefontaine in July 2017—when behind stablemate at the time Beau Gosse, who is now borderline smart for Guillaume Macaire—and that already looks money well spent after a brief campaign in novice company last winter, winning two of his three outings in the space of six weeks.

An opening sixth in the mud at Sandown (2m) in December proved much stronger form than it perhaps looked at the time—five of the 10 runners in that novice won next-time-out—and Greaneteen has arguably come as far as any from that race since, having signed off with back-to-back wins in a maiden at Exeter and a novice at Fontwell, both at around 2¼m in January. He was very professional in the way that he completed the task on the first occasion, beating 17 rivals with the minimum of fuss, and it didn't take much in the way of improvement for him to follow up under a penalty next time, edging a tight finish with a performance that was backed up by the clock (excellent timefigure).

Off the track since, the handicapper has also taken a high view of what he achieved, with further improvement likely to be required if he is going to defy an opening mark of 134 over hurdles. That is certainly not beyond the realms of possibility given his unexposed profile, but it is for what he might achieve if switching to fences that he is included in the *Fifty*. Indeed, he looks just the sort of horse who should take well to chasing, a sound jumper of a hurdle with a rangy physique, and there is no finer man than Paul Nicholls to help him take his form to a new level over the larger obstacles, with the list of previous examples seemingly an endless one. **Paul Nicholls**

Conclusion: *Plenty to like about his attitude when winning his final two starts over hurdles and looks sure to go on to better things over fences this term*

Harambe   h136

6 br.g. Malinas (Ger) – Crystal Princess (Ire) (Definite Article)
2018/19 h16s^bd h16g² h20.5s⁴ h16.3d⁴ h16s* h18.6g* h16g² Apr 27

Harambe could hardly have laid down better foundations for hurdling in bumpers, winning on debut at Ludlow prior to an excellent third in a Grade 2 at Aintree's Grand National Festival in April 2018. Circumstances then conspired against him to start with over obstacles, his list of excuses on his first four outings being as follows (in chronological order); brought down, stuck behind a loose horse, too free upped to 21f and held up in a steadily-run race. It did finally click when Harambe landed a 2m novice at Kempton in March, and he was even more impressive when following up under a penalty over 19f at Market Rasen the following month, improving again to win by nine lengths.

Given Harambe's free-going ways, a big-field handicap scenario was always going to see him to maximum effect, and he duly took his form to a new level when runner-up to the exciting prospect—and fellow *Fifty* qualifier—Getaway Trump in a 15-runner event back over 2m at Sandown on his final start, ultimately ending a season that started slowly in very positive fashion.

Harambe has the makings of a useful novice chaser if and when connections opt for that route, though he still had some filling out to do when last seen (tall, rather unfurnished gelding), and, with that in mind, it's not the greatest surprise that connections are reportedly leaning towards continuing over hurdles with him this season, with the Greatwood Hurdle volunteered as an early-season target. The way that race is likely to be run should play to his strengths, and with a BHA mark of 137 still appealing as fair, he is not to one to take lightly for that race and beyond. ***Alan King***

Conclusion: *Good-quality bumper performer who made a sticky start to life over hurdles but came good in the spring; may yet have more to offer if settling better in strongly-run 2m handicaps*

Highland Hunter (Ire) ★   h130p

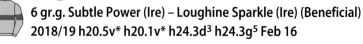

6 gr.g. Subtle Power (Ire) – Loughine Sparkle (Ire) (Beneficial)
2018/19 h20.5v* h20.1v* h24.3d³ h24.3g⁵ Feb 16

A winning pointer, Highland Hunter's only defeat in his first four starts under Rules occurred in a Grade 2 bumper at Aintree in 2018, and, having made a successful hurdling debut at Ayr last November, to say that he was backed off the boards under a penalty at Hexham the following month wouldn't be an understatement—he was sent off 3/1-on when seeing off a fellow-penalised runner who boasted comparable form, if not potential, going into the race. He then went like the best horse at the weights when third from a BHA mark of 128 on his handicap debut at Haydock in January, a shade too free tackling 3m for the first time and doing well under the circumstances to be beaten just a length and a half, only run out of it close home. There's substance to that form, too, with no fewer than four next-time-out winners in behind Highland Hunter that day.

Absent since finishing fifth in the Prestige Novices' Hurdle back at Haydock in February, when he wasn't seen to best effect (needs more emphasis on stamina), Highland Hunter has now moved south of the border from Lucinda Russell, and a BHA mark of 131 looks generous to say the least. Already proven over 3m, a slight drop in trip would do him no harm given how he goes about his business, and, yet to encounter a proper end-to-end gallop, Highland Hunter could easily take his form to a whole new level this season. He's been kept away from quick ground so far and certainly possesses the physique to excel over the larger obstacles. *Paul Nicholls*

Conclusion: *Sturdy gelding who showed considerable promise in four hurdling starts in 2018/19; joined the champion trainer in the interim and has plenty of options for this season, still potentially well treated over hurdles and with the physique to jump a fence*

Hill Sixteen   h119
6 b.g. Court Cave (Ire) – Chasers Chic (Karinga Bay)
2018/19 h20g³ h20.1s² h19.5s² h19.9d² h19.3g* h19.9v⁴ Mar 16

Trevor Hemmings has another fine prospect on his hands in the shape of the Sue Smith-trained Hill Sixteen. The six-year-old is a typical staying chaser in the making for his three-time Grand National-winning owner and it was all positive over hurdles last season.

Bought for £100,000 after winning his sole start in points, Hill Sixteen contested some strong novice events upon joining this yard, notably finishing third behind One For Rosie (now Timeform-rated 138) and subsequent Kingmaker Novice's Chase winner Glen Forsa on his hurdling debut at Carlisle last November. Hill Sixteen then filled the runner-up spot in each of his next three starts, producing his best effort when chasing home the promising Present Value at Chepstow on the second of them, and a deserved success finally came his way when returning to Carlisle in February, hitting the front after two out and asserting strongly thereafter to beat Vis A Vis by two and three quarter lengths. Allotted an opening mark of 123 on the back of that performance, Hill Sixteen was pitched in deep for his handicap debut at Uttoxeter in March—a 0-150 contest on Midlands National day—and, despite losing a shoe in the race, he ran creditably to finish fourth in very testing conditions.

Hill Sixteen will be found much easier opportunities than that from his current mark and is likely to stay 3m (yet to race beyond 2½m), which provides him with more options if continuing over hurdles. There are certainly handicaps to be won with him if that is the chosen path, though his profile and connections suggest that a switch to fences may be in the offing sooner rather than later. *Sue Smith*

Conclusion: *Lightly-raced sort whose hurdles form stacks up well; future lies over fences and longer trips but has a lenient mark to exploit in handicaps over the smaller obstacles before that*

Iconic Muddle h108p

6 gr.g. Sixties Icon – Spatham Rose (Environment Friend)
2018/19 h16.3s h16.3s :: 2019/20 h17.7g² May 8

England's Super Over victory against New Zealand at Lord's in July has already been written into cricket folklore, but the 50-over tie between South Africa v Australia in 1999 rivals it for drama. Needing just one further run to win from the final three balls at Edgbaston, Allan Donald and Lance Klusener got in an almighty muddle and both ended up at the same end, resulting in a run-out that scuppered South Africa's World Cup hopes at the semi-final stage (group-stage finishing positions was the metric used in event of a tie at that tournament).

Iconic Muddle almost certainly wasn't named after that piece of sporting drama given that his connections employ Muddle in names frequently. From a family his owners know well, among Iconic Muddle's four winning siblings is Not Another Muddle, who developed into a useful chaser for Gary Moore.

Too green to show much in a brace of maiden hurdles at Newbury three weeks apart last winter, Iconic Muddle left that form well behind when chasing home Some Day Soon in a Fontwell maiden in May, never nearer than the two and a half lengths that he was beaten at the line. The most salient part of that performance is that Jamie Snowden's six-year-old has since gone on to complete a four-timer, and though he was undoubtedly placed to good effect, it's still form to be positive about (Some Day Soon currently rated 130 with Timeform). On that evidence, Iconic Muddle's opening BHA mark of 115 is a more than fair assessment, and given Gary Moore's typical approach, there is probably still a bit to work on, with trips around 2½m also likely to see him to even better effect.
Gary Moore

Conclusion: *Took a significant step forward on his final 2018/19 start, form that has since been well advertised by the winner; still an unexposed quantity heading into modest handicap company*

Imperial Aura (Ire) h131p

6 b.g. Kalanisi (Ire) – Missindependence (Ire) (Executive Perk)
2018/19 h19.3g* h20.6g* Feb 23

Kim Bailey is perhaps best known for winning both the Champion Hurdle (Alderbrook) and Gold Cup (Master Oats) at the 1995 Cheltenham Festival, but there has also been plenty to be positive about in more recent campaigns, with the trainer breaking the 50-winner barrier for the second time in five seasons in 2018/19. Bailey looks to have assembled a strong team to go to war with this season, too, and he is likely to be particularly excited about Imperial Aura, who contributed two wins from his only appearances during the last campaign.

Imperial Aura has been beaten only once in four starts, in a hot Kempton bumper on debut in February 2018, and having landed the odds at Ludlow in April of that year, he was well supported to make a winning return starting out over hurdles at Carlisle last autumn. He took time to warm to his task on that occasion, the sharp nature of the course possibly against him, but he drew clear in the closing stages to win by three and a quarter lengths from Sole Pretender, who now boasts a Timeform rating of 149. Imperial Aura wasn't seen again until February, but he brushed the absence aside with an impressive display over 2½m at Newcastle, looking better the further he went on that galloping track, leading on the bridle after three out and always in command thereafter.

Imperial Aura remains with tons of potential, and it will be interesting to see whether he goes handicapping over hurdles or if his wily trainer quickly switches him to chasing, which is surely when he'll come into his own. *Kim Bailey*

Conclusion: *Smart prospect who has the option of handicap hurdles or novice chases in 2019/20, sure to win more races whatever path he takes*

King Roland (Ire)   b116p

5 br.g. Stowaway – Kiltiernan Robin (Ire) (Robin des Champs (Fr))
2018/19 b15.8v* b15.8s* Feb 26

The second exciting and unbeaten prospect for Harry Fry in the *Fifty* after Get In The Queue, King Roland oozes class, and it will be disappointing if he doesn't take high rank among the novice hurdlers this season.

A €40,000 purchase as a three-year-old, there were signs right from the start that King Roland could be something out of the ordinary as he breezed to a 10-length win in a 3m maiden point at Larkhill in March 2018 before joining Harry Fry. Sent off 11/8-on for his bumper debut at Uttoxeter nine months on, the hooded King Roland blew his eight rivals away with a stunning show of strong galloping in the mud, storming clear in the straight for a 22-length success. That resulted in a Timeform rating of 116, right up there with the best bumper performances in Britain throughout last season, and even more impressive given that it was his first start under Rules.

King Roland made his second start in bumpers at Ffos Las in February—just four days after Get In The Queue had posted a figure of 119 in winning at Exeter—and he again impressed in testing conditions as he landed odds of 9/4-on with a comfortable victory, beating Stick With Bill by a length with a bit in hand. He cruised into contention from well off the pace approaching the home turn, and having taken it up entering the final furlong, responded well to Fehily's urgings to maintain his advantage. King Roland will have learned plenty from that experience, and having missed the spring festival bumpers, he'll likely feature among the best recruits to novice hurdles in 2019/20. *Harry Fry*

Conclusion: *Unbeaten in a point and two bumpers and looks a fantastic prospect for novice hurdles*

Lostintranslation (Ire) ★   c160p

7 b.g. Flemensfirth (USA) – Falika (Fr) (Hero's Honor (USA))
2018/19 c22.4d² c19.9d³ c20.6d* c20s² c19.8d² c25d* Apr 5

If there is one chaser in this season's *Fifty* who could go right to the top, it is undoubtedly Lostintranslation, a smart novice hurdler in 2017/18 who enjoyed a tremendous campaign when quickly switched to fences last term. He chased home the excellent mare La Bague Au Roi at Newbury on his first two outings, before opening his chase account in the Dipper Novices' Chase at Cheltenham on New Year's Day, getting the better of the 2017 Triumph Hurdle winner Defi du Seuil by a length and a quarter. That rival would have the upper hand subsequently in the Scilly Isles Novices' Chase at Sandown and JLT Novices' Chase at Cheltenham, but Lostintranslation emerged with both his rating and reputation enhanced, again putting in an exemplary round of jumping at the Festival but just unable to live with Defi du Seuil's turn of foot on the run-in.

Lostintranslation was upped in trip to 25f for the Mildmay Novices' Chase at Aintree on his final start, the result being a hugely-impressive display as he jumped his rivals into the ground, beating the odds-on Topofthegame by six lengths. On that evidence, he may yet prove capable of better when stamina is at even more of a premium, with the Ladbrokes Trophy at Newbury—a race that his trainer has won twice in the last three years—very much appealing as a suitable starting point. In any case, there is an overwhelming feeling

Lostintranslation developed into a high-class novice chaser last season

that Lostintranslation hasn't reached his limit, and he looks set to take high rank among the staying chasers in 2019/20, with the Gold Cup likely to be the ultimate aim. **Colin Tizzard**

Conclusion: *Really likeable type who quickly made up into a high-class chaser last season and looks set to do even better as his stamina is drawn out further*

Mcfabulous (Ire)   b116

5 b.g. Milan – Rossavon (Ire) (Beneficial)
2018/19 b16d* b16.4g b16.3d* b17d* Apr 5

A half-brother to the useful hurdler/top-class chaser Waiting Patiently, as well as the useful hurdler Walking In The Air, it has to go down as seriously encouraging that McFabulous possessed the pace to win three bumpers last season, including the Grade 2 at Aintree (running to a Timeform figure of 116 in the process) in April.

A blip at Cheltenham aside (when reportedly returning with sore shins), McFabulous has passed each test to date with flying colours, the first of which came when comfortably beating fellow *Fifty* member Ask Dillon at Chepstow in October, with Lisnagar Oscar, who would prove himself a useful hurdler by the end of the campaign, providing further substance to the form in third. McFabulous was then given time to recover from his Cheltenham flop and bounced back in emphatic fashion at Newbury in early-March, winning by six lengths with one of the best bumper performances of the season to that point, before bringing up win number three in much deeper waters at the Grand National meeting, asserting in the final furlong to get the verdict by a length.

The runner-up that day Thebannerkingrebel has since won both starts over hurdles, and there is no doubt that McFabulous has all the makings of a smart performer when going down that route himself this season. Given his pedigree, the Ballymore Novices' Hurdle is perhaps the most likely destination for him if making it to the Cheltenham Festival, and, while trainer Paul Nicholls can boast plenty of strength in depth in this division, few are likely to have him as excited as McFabulous. **Paul Nicholls**

Conclusion: *Created excellent impression in winning three of his four bumper starts and has to be high on the shortlist among the best prospects for novice hurdles this season; likely to stay 2½m*

Mister Fisher (Ire)   h143p

5 b.g. Jeremy (USA) – That's Amazing (Ire) (Marignan (USA))
2018/19 h16.3d² h16g* h15.7d* h16.4s :: 2019/20 h15.7g May 11

Mister Fisher's entry in the 2018/19 edition of this publication signed off with the sentence: *'Mister Fisher is expected to take high rank in the novice hurdling division.'* In the event, that statement proved not too far wide of the mark, given that he was sent off 14/1 for the Supreme Novices' Hurdle (ultimately finishing eighth) following useful wins in a novice at Kempton and the Rossington Main Novices' Hurdle at Haydock (by two and a half lengths from Bright Forecast, who has also made the cut for this year's *Fifty*).

Mister Fisher was allotted a mark of 145 for his handicap debut in the Swinton Handicap Hurdle at Haydock in May, and he made a pleasing start to life in that sphere by finishing seventh, his relative lack of big-field experience just counting against him on the day, still likely to have finished closer than the seven lengths he was beaten but for a blunder at the last (tied up in the final 100 yards). That experience is unlikely to have been lost on him, and, that being the case, he is one to look out for in valuable early-season pots, with the Greatwood Hurdle at Cheltenham in November a possible target. He has been raced exclusively at 2m to date but is likely to stay further on breeding. **Nicky Henderson**

Conclusion: *Quickly developed into a useful novice hurdler last season and is one to bear in mind for high-end handicaps at up to 2½m*

Mister Malarky c149

6 ch.g. Malinas (Ger) – Priscilla (Teenoso (USA))
2018/19 c19.7g* c23.4s³ c23.4d* c23.8d* c24.4s⁴ c25g² Apr 6

We've already touched upon Colin Tizzard's superb knack when it comes to improving chasers from a relatively-low base, and Mister Malarky certainly fits that bill having blossomed in six starts over the larger obstacles last term, improving on his hurdles rating to the tune of 33 lb on our scale, culminating in an excellent second (five lengths behind Kildisart) in a Grade 3 handicap at Aintree's Grand National Festival. Needless to say, that is the trajectory of an upwardly-mobile chaser, and where that line will plateau in just his second season over fences remains to be seen.

It's also well worth pointing out that, following his reappearance success at Plumpton, Mister Malarky tackled fences at exclusively Grade-1 tracks, with the way that his jumping stood up to those tests auguring extremely well for the future. As far as targets go, there's no question that Mister Malarky will stay marathon trips, and it wouldn't be a major surprise were he to run in the Grand National either this season or next, with the same route taken by stablemate Elegant Escape (and Native River before him) last season—the Ladbrokes Trophy at Newbury followed by the Welsh Grand National at Chepstow—appealing as one that would make plenty of sense before the turn of the year.

Admittedly, Elegant Escape was rather found out for speed at Newbury before relishing the extra emphasis on stamina in Wales, and Mister Malarky is very much in the same mould, with his best days likely to come when encountering 3½m+. He acts on heavy going—which could come in handy if heading to Chepstow—and it's worth reiterating that he has looked a thoroughly sound jumper of fences, an asset that will continue to stand him in good stead in some of the season's major staying handicap chases. **Colin Tizzard**

Conclusion: *Reliable sort who made giant strides in his first season over fences and could yet climb higher still when tackling marathon trips (looks a thorough stayer)*

Phil Thompson (Mister Malarky): *"Few horses in recent memory have looked as well suited by the switch to chasing than Colin Tizzard's Mister Malarky, who made massive strides in his first season over fences, winning three times (including at graded level) before signing off with good efforts at two of the major spring festivals. Despite winning over 2½m last term, he's looked all about stamina and, with the prospect of even more to come over extreme trips, he rates a major contender for some of the more valuable long-distance handicap chases in 2019/20."*

Molly The Dolly (Ire) c144p

8 b.m. Flemensfirth (USA) – Pistol Flash (Ire) (Pistolet Bleu (Ire))
2018/19 c25g* c24g* c23.4s³ c24.1m* Apr 13

It's hard to think of a more upwardly-mobile trainer in the National Hunt ranks than Dan Skelton, with a cursory glance at his season totals reading 27, 73, 104, 118 and 156 prior to a superb 205 wins last term—you have to go back to the Martin Pipe juggernaut of the 1990s for the last time that a British jumps trainer broke the 200-winner barrier. The quantity over quality tag associated with the yard is probably a harsh one, too, with Roksana a first Grade 1 winner (albeit in fortuitous fashion) for team Skelton in the OLBG Mares' Hurdle back in the spring. That is highly likely to be just the first of many top-level wins for the Warwickshire handler, and while Molly The Dolly is probably not quite up to that class, the commanding performance she put in to win in handicap company on her final start at Ayr in April marks her out as a very useful mare to go to war with in her own right.

A mare of Molly The Dolly's class can be placed to good advantage against her own sex, with listed races at Newbury and Huntingdon appealing as suitable targets around the turn of the year. It's worth remembering that Magic of Light, who won the former race last season before ultimately finishing second in the Grand National, went into the campaign with a lower Timeform rating than Molly The Dolly, while stablemate Rene's Girl won twice in listed mares' chases back in 2017/18. That is not to say that Molly The Dolly cannot hold her own in open handicap company from a BHA mark in the mid-140s, either, with the prospect of even better to come (still low mileage for an eight-year-old), and it will be disappointing if there aren't races of some description to be won with her this season, with no better man for spying a winnable opportunity than Skelton. ***Dan Skelton***

Conclusion: *Lightly-raced mare who took form to a new level over fences last season (winning three of four starts) and could be a big factor in listed races against her own sex this term*

 Follow us on Twitter @Timeform

Precious Cargo (Ire) h136p

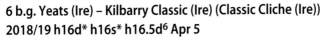

6 b.g. Yeats (Ire) – Kilbarry Classic (Ire) (Classic Cliche (Ire))
2018/19 h16d* h16s* h16.5d⁶ Apr 5

By Yeats and the first foal of a bumper winner, it wasn't a huge surprise that Precious Cargo was up to making a successful debut for Lucinda Russell at Ayr in January 2018, but the manner of the victory certainly raised a few eyebrows, readily seeing off the standard-setting Sao Mexence by 11 lengths, with another 13 lengths back to a next-time-out winner in third.

The deep impression he created that day made it all the more disappointing that he was unable to add to his tally in two further starts in bumpers, and a lot of water went under the bridge before we saw him back on a racecourse after nine months off at Kempton, where he started out in novice company over hurdles after both a breathing operation—it's worth noting that he had worn a tongue tie in his three starts in bumpers—and a change of scenery, making his first appearance for Nicky Henderson at the Sunbury venue. Which of those adjustments had the greatest influence is hard to know, but, whatever the cause, Precious Cargo was right back to looking the good prospect he had appeared on debut, winning readily by three and a quarter lengths, and even more encouraging was that he was able to put two good runs together by scoring just as impressively on his next start at Sandown, defying a penalty by eight lengths with the minimum of fuss.

A tilt at the Top Novices' Hurdle at Aintree on his final start ultimately proved a bridge too far at that stage of Precious Cargo's career, but it's worth pointing out that he still looked on the weak side throughout last season (rather unfurnished sort), and a mistake when trying to close two out really seemed to knock the stuffing out of him. He remains with potential, especially with another summer to strengthen under his belt, and it would be no surprise if he proved a totally different proposition this time round, be that as a second-season hurdler or a novice chaser. **Nicky Henderson**

Conclusion: *Useful-looking gelding who is expected to flourish in his second season, presumably over hurdles, though a switch to fences wouldn't be a major surprise given his build*

Pym (Ire) h127

6 b.g. Stowaway – Liss Rua (Ire) (Bob Back (USA))
2018/19 h16d* h15.7m² h21g² h21d* h20.3d Mar 15

One of the most interesting talking points ahead of the 2019/20 National Hunt campaign is the route that Altior will take in his quest to extend a winning sequence currently standing at 19, with the outstanding 2m chaser of the last three seasons reportedly set to go up in trip for races such as the King George. It's very rare to see a horse find as much for pressure as Altior, and while his pedigree doesn't necessarily scream 3m, his run style certainly does. It's certainly something for owner Patricia Pugh to ponder, and while another of her representatives, Pym, doesn't share his ability, there is at least less doubt about his ability to thrive when going up in trip this season.

A bumper winner on debut back in April 2017, Pym emulated his illustrious stablemate in landing a 2m novice at Chepstow on his hurdling debut the following October. He then produced even better efforts in defeat when filling the runner-up spot at Ascot (2m) and Cheltenham (21f Grade 2), both in November, and there was plenty to like about the way he battled to resume winning ways at Kempton (21f) two months later, responding well to give weight and a beating to a fairly useful stablemate.

It's fair to say that Pym is probably a notch or two below the top table, but his pedigree points to further progress when he is stepped up to 3m, being a Stowaway half-brother to three winners, including the fairly useful hurdlers Beneagles (25f winner) and Minella Aris (3m winner). The way that he shaped on his final start in the 21f Martin Pipe at the Cheltenham Festival was also indicative of one wanting to go up in trip (outpaced after two out before making some late gains), and a good example of what Pym may be able to achieve comes in the form of another Henderson inmate, Thomas Campbell—he raised his game significantly in winning a brace of Cheltenham handicaps at up to 25f on his first two starts back in 2017/18, and connections may well chart a similar course with Pym. **Nicky Henderson**

Conclusion: *Always been held in high regard and could be about to justify that belief when stepping up to 3m in handicaps this season, potentially a useful stayer in the making*

Queenohearts (Ire)   h133p
6 ch.m. Flemensfirth (USA) – Chars (Ire) (Old Vic)
2018/19 h19.5s² h18.9v* h19.8s* h16.8d Mar 14

'My dear, here we must run as fast as we can, just to stay in place. And if you wish to go anywhere you must run twice as fast as that.'

That famous quote was first uttered by the Queen of Hearts in Lewis Carroll's classic Alice's Adventures in Wonderland, and it seems even more relevant in the fast-paced modern world where merely maintaining standards won't suffice. Thankfully for Queenoheart's connections, her progression through the ranks has been a relentless one to date, and with staying trips still to explore, it would be no surprise if she continued in that vein in the months ahead.

Back-to-back bumper wins in 2017/18—latterly in listed company at Sandown—marked Queenohearts down as an above-average recruit to hurdling, as if her pedigree didn't already (by Flemensfirth and out of an unraced half-sister to the top-class hurdler Macs Joy). A runner-up effort in maiden company at Chepstow (19f) last November was a more than satisfactory start, finishing directly ahead of three next-time-out winners, and she did her bit for the form of that race when winning her next two outings, in a listed mares' novice at Haydock in December and the Grade 2 Jane Seymour Mares' Novices' Hurdle at Sandown in February. She was forced to concede 5 lb all round on the latter occasion but proved well up to the task, clearly not held back by a slightly awkward head carriage as she asserted on the run-in to beat Danse Idol by two and a quarter lengths with a bit in hand.

Connections may lament running Queenohearts in the Dawn Run Mares' Novices' Hurdle at the Cheltenham Festival, given that the extended 2m trip was clearly far too sharp for her, and, with the benefit of hindsight, she probably would have been better off contesting the 2½m Mares' Hurdle 48 hours earlier, with a Timeform rating of just 123 needed to make the first four in that more valuable race. Nevertheless, defeat in the Dawn Run didn't preclude stable flagbearer Maria's Benefit from developing into a useful chaser (remains with potential) last term, and very similar comments apply to Queenohearts going into the new campaign, a lengthy mare who has not yet had the platform to show all that she can, a step up to 3m likely to see her improve again. **Stuart Edmonds**

Conclusion: *Gained some valuable black type over hurdles last term and may not have finished yet, with a step up to 3m likely to see her in an even better light over fences*

Paul Goodenough (Queenohearts**):** *"Given the expansion of opportunities in recent years for good-quality mares, and with one eye on the addition of a new race over fences at next season's Cheltenham Festival, the future looks bright for Queenohearts, who has already shown useful form over hurdles when beating a host of subsequent winners in a Sandown Grade 2 event for novices, though everything about her suggests that we've merely scratched the surface with her ability-wise, the step up to 3m and/or a switch to chasing likely to reap rewards in what generally looks a weak division, at least on this side of the Irish Sea."*

Reserve Tank (Ire) ★   h150p
5 b.g. Jeremy (USA) – Lady Bellamy (Ire) (Black Sam Bellamy (Ire))
2018/19 h16d³ h16.3d h16s* h21s* h20g* h20d* May 3

Top-class chaser Denman—who flamboyant part-owner Harry Findlay dubbed *'The Tank'* in tribute to his size and powerful, relentless running style—was always going to improve markedly for the switch to fences, and while Reserve Tank has a job on trying to scale the same heights as the 2008 Cheltenham Gold Cup winner, the future is certainly very bright as he makes his own transition to chasing this term.

Whereas Denman seemed to have a huge reputation right from the very start, Reserve Tank's progress in his first season over hurdles came as more of a surprise, at least as far as punters were concerned; indeed, he wasn't even favourite for either of his soft-ground novice wins at Sandown (2m) in February and Kempton (21f) in March, while the promise of those efforts was ignored to an extent when he lined up in the 2½m Mersey Novices' Hurdle at Aintree in April, going off 20/1 in a field of nine. That mattered little on the day, though, as he found further progress to take the step up in class in his stride, beating the useful Brewin'upastorm by three and a quarter lengths despite a mistake at the last.

Sent off 13/2 for the Champion Novices' Hurdle at Punchestown (also over 2½m) on his final start, Reserve Tank strengthened his status as one of the best young prospects around by improving still further to follow up from Aintree. He impressed most with how he travelled, and only a little less with how he jumped, while the way that he put his head down when challenged after the last was equally encouraging for one still relatively short on experience, finding plenty to beat Sams Profile by half a length.

A quick switch to novice chasing is on the agenda for Reserve Tank this term, and he certainly possesses the necessary attributes to be a leading player in that division, an imposing sort physically who usually travels strongly in his races. He's not short of speed, either, though the evidence of his novice hurdling campaign suggests that the intermediate trip of the JLT Novices' Chase will prove more up his street than the 2m of the Arkle at the Cheltenham Festival. **Colin Tizzard**

Conclusion: *Created an excellent impression in winning his final four starts over hurdles, including a pair of Grade 1s, and looks destined to enjoy further success in graded novice chases*

Reserve Tank (blue) is expected to take high rank amongst the novice chasers this term

Second Time Around
c117

7 b.g. Midnight Legend – Silk Rope (Ire) (Presenting)
2018/19 h19.6g^4 h23.3g^2 h26.4m^5 c19.9d^2 c20.5d^F c21.4g^3 Mar 27

Shalamar probably had other things in mind when singing the lyrics '*the second time is so much better baby*' in their 1979 hit The Second Time Around, but connections of this son of Midnight Legend will be very much hoping that that sentiment rings true in his second season over fences, having failed to pull up any trees at the first attempt.

Although a bumper winner at Market Rasen back in 2017, Second Time Around has frankly looked rather slow over obstacles, ultimately failing to add to that success in 10 subsequent starts. There was always the strong feeling that chasing would be his game given his looks and pedigree—he is a lengthy gelding whose dam is a half-sister to the very smart chaser (stayed 2½m) Defy Logic and out of an unraced half-sister to the top-class chaser Strong Promise—and Second Time Around attracted plenty of support (sent off 9/4 and 3/1) in his first two starts over fences. In the event, however, it was jumping blemishes that had his followers cursing their luck, closing in behind the all-the-way winner when belting two out at Huntingdon (2½m) in December, and then falling before the race could take shape at Kempton (20.5f) the following month. He put in a better round when third at Market Rasen (21f) in March on his final start, but still didn't enjoy the rub of the green as might have been hoped, keeping on when short of room at the last (beaten only two and a half lengths at the line).

Second Time Around is by no means the most talented member of our *Fifty*, but he looks sure to prove capable of better than he has shown so far over fences when returned to 3m, with his best effort over hurdles having come over 23f. Going that bit slower over longer might just help him to brush up his jumping, too, and with his novice status still intact, he can surely be placed to win a race by his expert handler.
Alan King

Conclusion: *Remains open to more improvement after only three starts over fences, especially when stepping up to 3m+, and should be up to winning his share of low-level handicaps*

Secret Investor
c147p

7 b.g. Kayf Tara – Silver Charmer (Charmer)
2018/19 h24.5g* h19.5d* c20.2g^2 c24g^2 c20.5g^4 c20.2g* c20.5m* Apr 13

Secret Investor was purchased for £175,000 in 2016 after winning his only start in Irish maiden points, but he didn't exactly hit the ground running when sent hurdling, finishing runner-up on four of his first five starts (seemingly amiss the other occasion). A hat-trick of hurdle wins followed, however, and he looked the real deal when completing the three-timer in a Grade 2 novice event at Chepstow last October on the back of a five-month break and a breathing operation (hardly the first from the stable to come on a ton after wind surgery).

The good-bodied Secret Investor always promised to make a better chaser, given his pointing background and physical presence, and he immediately ran to a higher level the moment he was switched to the larger obstacles, though he was again thrown in at the deep end and, mirroring his early hurdles career, had to wait for his fourth start before getting his head in front. Following that confidence-boosting, 20-length success in an ordinary novice event at Wincanton, Secret Investor was quickly stepped back up in grade for the seven-runner Future Champions Novices' Chase at Ayr, and he finished his first season chasing in the style that it was expected to start, finally looking the real deal again in winning by three and three quarter lengths, well on top at the finish.

There's no reason why Secret Investor won't take that late momentum into his second season as a chaser. There's talk of him starting off in the Grade 2 Skymas Chase at Down Royal in November, but he's a versatile individual, effective anywhere between 2½m–3m, and there will also be plenty of opportunities for him in high-end handicaps. *Paul Nicholls*

Conclusion: *Ended novice season over fences firmly on the upgrade and looks the sort to go on again for a yard with few peers when it comes to the handling of developing chasers*

Secret Investor remains with potential over fences

Shut The Box (Ire)   h114p

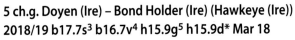

5 ch.g. Doyen (Ire) – Bond Holder (Ire) (Hawkeye (Ire))
2018/19 b17.7s³ b16.7v⁴ h15.9g⁵ h15.9d* Mar 18

The bumper in which Shut The Box finished third at Fontwell in April 2018 wasn't an obvious contest to keep an eye on at the time, but it actually worked out really well, with the runner-up Itchy Feet finishing third in the Supreme Novices' Hurdle the following March, while the fourth Flic Ou Voyou won his next two starts at Wincanton (posted a useful effort in defying a penalty on the latter occasion). Chris Gordon's inmate didn't really do his bit for the form of that race in two subsequent bumper starts over longer trips, but he duly built on the promise of his hurdling debut at Plumpton when landing the odds back at that track in March.

Being the second foal out of a half-sister to the fair hurdler/useful chaser (stayed 31f) Sizing Australia and the useful hurdler/fairly useful chaser (stayed 3m) Frontier Dancer, there is every indication that Shut The Box will stay further on breeding, though he's looked an exuberant type so far, leaving the impression that a well-run handicap over 2m could be right up his alley, and the assessor cannot go overboard with the aforementioned Plumpton win, given that that race was effectively a match (runner-up Vision Clear didn't have to improve much to open his account at Kempton in May).

Representing the underrated Chris Gordon, who can boast a double-figure strike rate with his jumps runners each season since 2014-15, Shut The Box is expected to be placed to good effect, with the trainer often targeting races at Plumpton and Fontwell, but there's every reason to think that this son of Doyen can mix it in handicaps at the top-tier tracks. The mind-numbingly tedious Deal Or No Deal lasted over 10 years before Channel 4 finally decided to Shut The Box in 2016, but I would happily decline and press on if offered two wins as a return for 2019/20. **Chris Gordon**

Conclusion: *Cemented a positive start to his career when landing a maiden hurdle at Plumpton in March and looks the sort to relish a big-field handicap environment over 2m, or perhaps further given the stamina on the dam's side of the pedigree*

Siruh du Lac (Fr) ★   c147p

6 b.g. Turgeon (USA) – Margerie (Fr) (Le Balafre (Fr))
2018/19 c19.9d* c19.2s* c20.6d* c20.6d* Mar 14

Nick Williams' Siruh du Lac is reportedly quite fragile, which presumably explains why the six-year-old ran only four times last season, but he won all four, improving in leaps and bounds, and there's no telling where his progress may end.

With an overall record of six wins from seven completed starts over fences, Siruh du Lac seems to leave nothing on the track, giving whatever is asked of him and finding more and more as the tasks become increasingly stiffer. Having returned from nine months off last November, he gained a couple of routine wins in Class 3 handicaps before the turn of the year, both by less than two lengths, and then was stepped up to Grade 3 company on Cheltenham Trials Day, where he again jumped superbly and made most, rallying after the last to edge ahead again in the final 100 yards and beat Nicky Henderson's Janika by a head.

That pair reopposed in the 22-runner Brown Advisory & Merriebelle Stable Plate at the Cheltenham Festival, a contest for which Janika was weighted to turn the placings around, going off favourite to do so. In the event, however, Siruh du Lac was having none of it, once more showing what a truly magnificent jumper of fences he is, making every yard and demonstrating a wonderful never-say-die attitude as he was tackled from two out, having three quarters of a length to spare over his old adversary at the line.

Any horse who gives his all so willingly is more than entitled to a little rest between races, so don't expect to see Siruh du Lac turning out month after month, but if you get only one chance to go racing in the 2019/2020 season, go and see Lizzy Kelly and Siruh du Lac. Given his excellent record at the track, the BetVictor Gold Cup at Cheltenham's November meeting looks an obvious starting point, while, looking further ahead, he strikes as one who is tailor-made for the Topham Chase over the Grand National fences—what a spectacle that would be! *Nick Wiliams*

Conclusion: *Proved most progressive during a sparing campaign over fences in 2018/19 and should continue to be a force in high-end handicaps over intermediate trips from a BHA mark of 150*

Siruh du Lac (yellow cap) went unbeaten in four starts over fences last season

Sky Pirate   c135

6 b.g. Midnight Legend – Dancingwithbubbles (Ire) (Supreme Leader)
2018/19 h24.7g^3 h23g* h23g^3 c24g^2 c24.5d^2 c25gbd c24.2d^4 c26d Mar 14

It's a sign of the times that Jonjo O'Neill has only two representatives in this year's *Fifty*, but both Cloth Cap and Sky Pirate look to have what it takes to bring the glory days back to Jackdaws Castle. O'Neill sent out only 56 winners last season—his lowest total since the 1999/2000 campaign—and he had just four runners at the Cheltenham Festival, but it was there that Sky Pirate marked himself down as a handicap chaser to follow.

A £150,000 purchase in March 2017 after winning a point, Sky Pirate made up into a useful performer in six starts over hurdles, recording the second of his two wins from a BHA mark of 123, and he started life over fences with a pair of good seconds over 3m at Uttoxeter and Carlisle last autumn, immediately stepping up on the pick of his hurdling efforts. He was then pitched into a good amateur riders' handicap (25f) at the Cheltenham November meeting, where he would have been second at worst under Patrick Mullins had he stood up, travelling well and keeping on in a close fourth when brought down two out.

Sky Pirate again ran well when returning after three months off in a 3m novice handicap at Exeter, and further evidence that he is on a handy mark came when seventh in the 26f Kim Muir at the Festival on his final start. Still in third jumping the last, he simply failed to get home with the emphasis so firmly on stamina, ultimately tying up on the run-in and losing several places.

It's hard to believe Sky Pirate begins the new season as a maiden over fences given the ratings he's run to, but that will surely change in the near-future, and he's reportedly set to be dropped in trip, which looks a good move. An early return could be on the cards, and, if he were to gain that elusive win on his reappearance, then we could see him in the BetVictor Gold Cup back at Cheltenham's November meeting, a race his trainer has won in recent years with Johns Spirit and Taquin du Seuil. *Jonjo O'Neill*

Conclusion: *Useful hurdler who quickly made up into a better chaser and caught the eye in the Kim Muir on his final start; potentially well treated on a BHA mark of 132 and looks sure to win races over fences at up to 3m*

Slate House (Ire)   c129p

7 b.g. Presenting – Bay Pearl (Fr) (Broadway Flyer (USA))
2018/19 c19.7d^4 c19.9d^5 c19.9d^2 c15.9s Mar 12

It's fair to say that a rebuilding job is required to get Slate House back on track after a light first season over fences. A winning pointer in Ireland, he embarked on a Rules career with a big reputation, and maiden/Grade 2 victories at Cheltenham in the autumn of 2017 did nothing to dispel the theory that he'd end up smart, beating none other than the subsequent Supreme Novices' Hurdle winner Summerville Boy on the latter occasion, though he did rather enjoy the run of the race.

Highly tried later that season, Slate House failed to pass muster, but a switch to fences was expected to be the making of him given his physical scope (strong, good sort). He certainly showed an aptitude for chasing when fourth on his debut/reappearance in an unusually deep novice event at Plumpton (2½m) in January, his absence telling behind the classy French raider Master Dino, and he bounced back from a flop at Haydock (reportedly bled and underwent a breathing surgery afterwards) with his best effort when second at Newbury (2½m) in March, offering a good platform on which to build in going down by five lengths at the hands of the useful Huntsman Son.

Best not judged on his well-held eighth in the Arkle 10 days later (already struggling when hampered at the sixth), the suggestion is to wipe the '*slate*' clean and give this son of Presenting another chance over fences this term (novice status still intact), in the hope that he's campaigned at a slightly more realistic level. There are certainly races to be won if that does prove to be the case, with handicap options also to be explored from a BHA mark of 135. Slate House stays 2½m but is likely to prove best at shorter. **Colin Tizzard**

Conclusion: *Hasn't fulfilled early promise but highly tried along the way and should be winning races over fences this season in slightly calmer waters*

Sofia's Rock (Fr)　　　　　　　　　　h137p
5 b.g. Rock of Gibraltar (Ire) – Princess Sofia (UAE) (Pennekamp (USA))
2018/19 h16m* h16.5g³ h15.8d* :: 2019/20 h15.7g⁵ May 11

Sofia's Rock is predominantly bred for the Flat and cost €100,000 as a yearling. He probably didn't take all that long to name, being a son of Rock of Gibraltar out of the Pennekamp mare Princess Sofia, but it took him a while to find his feet on the Flat under the guidance of Mark Johnston, beaten at short odds on his first three starts before finally getting off the mark in a Class 5 maiden at Redcar on his final two-year-old outing. As his pedigree promised, however, he turned out to be useful in that sphere, winning Class 3 handicaps at Leicester and Haydock (twice), also excelling himself when a close third in a Group 3 at Newmarket somewhere in between.

Perhaps in spite of his pedigree, though, it looks like jumping hurdles could be the making of Sofia's Rock. He was transferred to Dan Skelton—invariably a move to sit up and take notice of—to embark on a hurdling career, and duly landed the odds in an ordinary maiden event at Worcester on his National Hunt bow last September. A five-month break and a breathing operation followed that debut, eventually returning with a much-improved performance in a Taunton novice hurdle, not winning but shaping really well having refused to settle in a race that wasn't run at an end-to-end gallop. Another large chunk of improvement ensued in a 10-runner novice at Ludlow the following month, a tongue tie possibly the catalyst, tanking along (but much more settled than at Taunton) and ultimately coming home an impressive 13-length winner having been eased close home.

The Swinton Handicap Hurdle looked the logical next step, and Sofia's Rock lost nothing in defeat at Haydock given his relative inexperience, building up a long lead and travelling with zest, headed only on landing at the last and, most significantly, showing himself to be a natural at jumping hurdles. Sofia's Rock's rate of improvement in four starts over timber has been stratospheric, albeit commensurate with the ability he showed on the Flat. He's always going to be seen to best advantage when speed, and fluent hurdling, is at a premium. **Dan Skelton**

Conclusion: *Came a long way in a short space of time over hurdles last term, quickly matching his useful Flat form, and highly likely to have handicaps in him from a BHA mark of 142 with the prospect of even more to come*

Soldier of Love   h114+

6 b.g. Yeats (Ire) – Monsignorita (Ire) (Classic Cliche (Ire))
2018/19 h16.7g³ h18.6s³ h19g² h23.9d* Feb 28

Given his stout pedigree (by Yeats and out of a half-sister to the fairly useful hurdler Cabinet Minister (stayed 25f)), it was most encouraging that Soldier of Love was able to finish runner-up in a six-runner bumper at Ascot on debut for Mark Pitman in November 2017, going down by just a neck despite showing clear signs of inexperience. A transfer to Fergal O'Brien followed on the back of Pitman's retirement, but he initially went backwards from that promising debut when lining up at Kempton four months later, proving far too keen for his good.

It was another seven months before we saw Soldier of Love on a racecourse again, and there was an element of laying the groundwork in his qualifying runs over hurdles at up to 19f, running to just a modest level on all three occasions. Those foundations—though uninspiring on the face of it—duly proved just that, with the combination of a switch to handicaps, the application of first-time cheekpieces and, perhaps most importantly, a step up to 3m all contributing to a much-improved showing when Soldier of Love was successful on his handicap debut (from an opening mark of 105) at Taunton in February, winning by six lengths. That race didn't really work out, but he was well on top at the line, and given the bumper figure he posted at Ascot, it would be a surprise if that proved his limit now that he's up and running.

Soldier of Love has a revised BHA mark of 113 to go to war with this season, and like Highland Hunter, he looks well weighted now embarking on life in new surroundings, having also made the switch to Paul Nicholls. Print businessman Malcolm Denmark has owned more talented horses (including the 2018 Grand National runner-up Pleasant Company in more recent times), but, from a modest base in handicap terms, there are surely a couple of staying handicaps with Soldier of Love's name on. **Paul Nicholls**

Conclusion: *Easy winner when up in trip/sporting first-time cheekpieces for his handicap debut at Taunton in February; since joined Paul Nicholls and totally unexposed as a stayer*

Sunshade ★   h138p

6 b.m. Sulamani (Ire) – Spring Flight (Groom Dancer (USA))
2018/19 h16.3d⁵ h20.3g* Apr 18

Sunshade did her early damage at relatively-unfashionable tracks back in 2017, but it all came very easily to her, landing a bumper at Fakenham before maintaining her unbeaten record with hurdling wins in a maiden at Ludlow (2m) and novice at Market Rasen (19f), giving 7 lb and a 14-length beating on the latter occasion to Black Sam Bella, who is now Timeform-rated 135p.

A step up to listed company proved too much too soon in December of the year, just too inexperienced to cope with the smart Maria's Benefit, and she has been restricted to only three runs since. Nevertheless, that made it all the more encouraging that she was able to build on the promise of her March reappearance when landing a 16-runner listed mares' handicap at Cheltenham (2½m) the following month, getting back on the up in no uncertain terms with a three and a half length defeat of an admirably consistent sort in the shape of Augusta Gold.

Timeform awarded Sunshade a rating of 138p on that back of that, a performance that suggests she is more than capable of competing outside of handicap company against her own sex, with listed races at up to 3m (should stay that far given how strong she was at the finish at Prestbury Park) likely to be on the agenda. Presumably not the easiest to keep sound, it's always a risk offering a mare like Sunshade as a horse to follow, but she has looked pretty good on the whole when making it to the track, and, granted a clear run of things, she could end up smart. ***Nicky Henderson***

Conclusion: *Lightly-raced mare who created excellent impression on final 2018/19 start and looks well up to mixing it against her own sex outside handicap company if getting a clearer run at her racing*

Talkischeap (Ire) ★   c155

7 b.g. Getaway (Ger) – Carrigmoorna Oak (Ire) (Milan)
2018/19 c22.4d³ c19.9d² c24g* c24d² c24g⁵ c28.8g* Apr 27

A useful performer in his only season over hurdles, Talkischeap bumped into La Bague Au Roi and Lostintranslation—both of whom would go on to win Grade 1 novice events later in the campaign—in each of his first two starts over fences at Newbury in November, still showing smart form in defeat, and he didn't need to improve to open his account in a match at Doncaster (3m) in January, ultimately doing so in straightforward fashion despite jumping out to his right on occasions.

His next two starts over 3m at Kempton didn't appear to get to the bottom of him, looking in need of further when fifth on his handicap debut in a valuable heat in February, and it was only when stepped up to 29f for the bet365 Gold Cup at Sandown in April that we really saw what he was made of, proving a BHA mark of 145 to be wholly inadequate, winning by 10 lengths from The Young Master and Step Back—both previous winners of the race—in emphatic fashion.

Talk is sometimes cheap, but the Timeform report following that win concluded: '*His sprint clear on the run-in was at total odds with the normal required tools of a long-distance chaser, a potent weapon that will ensure he remains of significant interest in good company next season, almost certainly starting in the Ladbrokes Trophy and perhaps culminating in a Grand National bid; in short, he's very much one to keep on the right side.*'

That analysis looks on the money at this stage, with those big targets also mooted by trainer Alan King, who landed the Newbury showpiece with Smad Place back in 2015. A revised BHA mark of 157 has been allocated to Talkischeap following that Sandown romp, but that is fully warranted when you factor in that he's still a seven-year-old who looked transformed by a well-run race over a marathon trip at Sandown. Such wide-margin winners in competitive races from marks in the mid-140s simply do not occur all that often, and it would be no surprise to see him break the mould even further this term. ***Alan King***

Talkischeap on his way to victory in the bet365 Gold Cup

Conclusion: *Improved no end for the step up to a marathon trip when an easy winner of the bet365 Gold Cup on his final start; remains open to more improvement and could be in for a big season, culminating in a tilt at the Grand National*

Top Ville Ben (Ire) c150

7 b.g. Beneficial – Great Decision (Ire) (Simply Great (Fr))
2018/19 c24.2s* c24.2d* c23.8d⁵ c24.4sᶠ c24.2d* c25d³ Apr 5

Regarded by many as an underrated trainer with the ammunition he has to work with, Phil Kirby raised the bar again in 2018/19 with an impressive 43 wins from 275 runners, a 16% strike rate also signalling career-best figures for the North Yorkshire handler (with a level-stake profit to boot). Lady Buttons continues to be the stable flagbearer, but Top Ville Ben more than held his own in what was a very productive novice season over fences.

Top Ville Ben's 2017/18 season ended with a heavy fall over hurdles, but he took superbly to the larger obstacles upon his return in the autumn, making all in novice company at Hexham and Wetherby (both at 3m). Further success beckoned at the latter venue in March, taking the aggregate winning margin for his three successes to 96 lengths, and though it wasn't always plain sailing for Top Ville Ben—he fell at the Cheltenham Festival and also jumped both left and right at times—he's already smart, with plenty to like about his uncomplicated way of going from the front, too.

Looking ahead to this season, Top Ville Ben appeals as the type to relish long-distance handicaps, and he's already well worth his place in a race like the Welsh National, his BHA rating up to 151 after his third behind fellow *Fifty* member Lostintranslation in the Mildmay Novices' Chase at Aintree in April. He can also make hay in graded company when he gets the opportunity to dominate in small but select fields, with the Charlie Hall Chase at his beloved Wetherby put forward as a potential early-season target, provided that there is a bit of ease underfoot; it's probably no coincidence that Top Ville Ben, who usually wears a hood, has so far been kept away from quick ground. ***Philip Kirby***

Conclusion: *Likeable front-runner who ended a fine novice season over fences with a good third in Grade 1 company at Aintree; highly likely to stay marathon trips and expected to pay his way again in high-end handicaps*

Whatsdastory (Ire) h103p

6 b.m. Beneficial – Supreme Contender (Ire) (Supreme Leader)
2019/20 h22.2g² May 13

Whatsdastory could end up being quite a familiar story if going the same way as the countless other horses who have transferred to the care of Dr Richard Newland from other yards. Indeed, the Worcestershire trainer has developed quite the reputation for turning around the fortunes of horses who have lost their way slightly, and those skills have been especially well advertised during the early stages of the current campaign—Newland saddled 29 winners up to the end of August, compared to the 53 that he recorded in the entire 2018/19 season.

Having also moved to a new *'top-of-the range'* facility in September, Newland is poised to kick on and make 2019/20 comfortably the best season of his training career to date, with Whatsdastory just one of several from the yard who looks a winner in waiting. Previously trained in Ireland by Debbie Hartnett, for whom she won a point, Whatsdastory showed plenty of ability when second on her Rules debut at Killarney in May, racing prominently and keeping on well to be beaten only three lengths in a mares' maiden hurdle that has thrown up its fair share of winners, with the third and fifth both advancing their form when winning similar events subsequently. That feat should prove a mere formality for Whatsdastory when starting out for her new connections this term, and while unlikely to be one of the stars of this year's *Fifty*, she looks just the sort that Newland will continue to extract improvement from, with 3m—and perhaps further—likely to prove her optimum trip on pedigree (dam an unraced sister to a pair of useful chasers who stayed 3m+). **Dr Richard Newland**

Conclusion: *Sure to improve on promising debut having joined shrewd connections in the interim and should win her fair share of races at a low level*

Whoshotthesheriff (Ire)　　　　　　　　　　h132

5 b.g. Dylan Thomas (Ire) – Dame Foraine (Fr) (Raintrap)
2018/19 b18.8d^2 b16d^3 h16s* h16d^2 h19.9s* h17m* Apr 20

With a record of three victories from four starts since embarking on a career over obstacles, Whoshotthesheriff has already achieved plenty, and it will be disappointing if he isn't able to improve further upon that fine record in the months ahead.

The son of Dylan Thomas is related to several National Hunt winners, and having run to a fair level in bumpers in Ireland, he upheld family honour with a successful switch to hurdling for his new owners at Ayr (2m) in January, returning from four months off with a comfortable success. Ridden by Sean Quinlan—who has partnered the five-year-old to all his wins—he was always travelling and jumping fluently, before staying on strongly to score by two and a half lengths, with another promising pair in Dali Mail and Sebastopol filling the places.

Whoshotthesheriff took another step forward on his next start at Navan (2m), despite meeting with defeat, beaten five lengths by the useful Galvin with mid-race errors not helping his cause. That proved to be his final start for Gordon Elliott, and it's fair to say that his move to Philip Kirby's yard could hardly have gone better so far. Stepped up to 2½m after nine weeks off at Sedgefield in March, Whoshotthesheriff overcame some late errors to double his hurdling tally, with the shoe he lost in the run possibly to blame for his tardiness over his obstacles as the race wore on, and a double penalty proved no barrier when back down in trip at Carlisle (17f) a month later, making it two from two in novice hurdles for Kirby with an easy success (by six lengths).

There are surely more races to be won with Whoshotthesheriff, and while he has the tempting option of handicap hurdles from a BHA mark of 130, he looks to have the physique to make a cracking chaser, with one of Timeform's finest judges describing him as *'a great big brute of a thing'*. **Philip Kirby**

Conclusion: *Won three of his four starts over hurdles in 2018/19, unbeaten in two for current connections; potentially well treated for handicaps over the smaller obstacles, but likely to be seen to best effect when jumping a fence*

Worthy Farm (Ire)   h125

6 b.g. Beneficial – Muckle Flugga (Ire) (Karinga Bay)
2018/19 h26g³ h23.9d* h24g h23.5d* h25.8g Mar 23

Much like racing enthusiasts and the Cheltenham Festival, the five days of the Glastonbury Festival are just about as good as it gets for music lovers. Not even knee-deep mud can stand in the way of their pilgrimage to the small Somerset village of Pilton, and over 200,000 people flocked to the most recent gathering held in late-June, with star names such as The Killers and Stormzy taking to the stage during a weekend when it felt like the eyes of the whole world were on Worthy Farm.

The equine Worthy Farm is yet to achieve quite the same level of recognition, but he is certainly in the right hands to maximise his potential on the racecourse; he is trained by Paul Nicholls, who has saddled over 3,000 winners from his Ditcheat yard—situated less than five miles from Worthy Farm—and celebrated winning his eleventh trainers' championship in 2018/19, a season in which Worthy Farm won two of his five starts over hurdles.

Third on his reappearance in a novices' hurdle at Warwick last November, Worthy Farm identified himself as one to follow all of a sudden when making a successful handicap debut at Taunton later that month, though his inexperience very nearly caused him to throw it away having looked in control on the run-in, hanging violently left entering the final 100 yards and allowing the runner-up to close within a neck. Worthy Farm then proved disappointing on his next start at Cheltenham, but he was right back to looking a very useful prospect when resuming winning ways in a 16-runner handicap at Ascot in February, making light of a 7 lb higher mark than at Taunton with a bit in hand. There was plenty of substance to that form, too, with Worthy Farm one of a quartet of second-season hurdlers filling the first four positions.

Still very raw throughout the last campaign—including when again failing to meet market expectations on his final start at Kelso—that can only bode well for the likelihood of further improvement this time round. Worthy Farm, a winning pointer, certainly has the physique of one who is likely to get better with age (good-topped gelding), and he is one to keep onside for his top yard in 2019/20, with plenty of mileage in his current mark if continuing down the handicapping route over hurdles. Worthy Farm stays 3¼m but may prove best at slightly shorter (recorded both wins to date at 3m). **Paul Nicholls**

Conclusion: *Shaped well amidst residual greenness last term and remains potentially well treated on a BHA mark of 130 over hurdles, with the scope to make a chaser, too*

Adam Houghton (Worthy Farm): *"Worthy Farm's antics in a couple of his races last season were reminiscent of a drunken gentleman staggering back to his tent after a session by the Pyramid Stage, but the hope is that he will be a reformed character when returning from his summer break. He has already demonstrated that there is plenty of ability hidden within his considerable frame when putting it all together, and while far from the headline act at Paul Nicholls' Ditcheat base, it will be a surprise if there aren't more good races to be won with him in the months ahead, with a switch to chasing likely to be the making of him when the time comes."*

SECTION

Allaho (Fr)   h138

5 b.g. No Risk At All (Fr) – Idaho Falls (Fr) (Turgeon (USA))
2018/19 b16g⁴ h24d* h24d³ h24d² May 1

As detailed in the write-up on Envoi Allen, we can expect to see the Cheveley Park Stud colours a lot more over jumps after their fantastic Cheltenham Festival double. The talent carrying their famous silks already runs much deeper than that pair of Festival heroes, and though beaten in the Albert Bartlett Novices' Hurdle at the same meeting, Allaho appeals as another whose best days are still ahead of him, with a switch to chasing sure to see him to better effect in the coming months.

Bought out of Guy Cherel's stable after finishing second in a listed hurdle at Auteuil on his debut in March 2018, Allaho was well backed on his first start for Willie Mullins in a bumper at Leopardstown on Boxing Day, but ultimately failed to meet expectations in fourth. It was an indicator of the regard in which he is held, though, that he returned to hurdles in a Grade 3 over 3m at Clonmel in February, and having clearly learned plenty from his first start in Ireland, he put in a very impressive performance to score by four lengths under Ruby Walsh, jumping fluently bar a clumsy error two out and staying on well to beat Minella Indo and a useful field containing five previous hurdles winners.

Allaho was one of three Mullins runners to line up in the Albert Bartlett at the Cheltenham Festival and the choice of Walsh. In the event, Minella Indo reversed Clonmel form with a surprise 33/1-success, but Allaho emerged with plenty of credit in third, beaten nine lengths with the two in front of him proving better suited by the emphasis on stamina. A third meeting with Henry de Bromhead's charge followed in the Irish Daily Mirror Novices' Hurdle at Punchestown, and, for all that Minella Indo prevailed once more, Allaho progressed again to get a good deal closer to his rival, keeping on well to be beaten only two lengths in second despite Walsh dropping his whip.

A cracking prospect for chasing, it would be no surprise to see Allaho improve past Minella Indo over fences this season. He proved at Punchestown that he stays 3m but will be just as effective back over shorter. *Willie Mullins*

Conclusion: *Showed himself useful in a short hurdling career and looks just the sort to do even better over fences this term, every inch a chaser on looks (strapping sort)*

Beacon Edge (Ire) b117p

5 b.g. Doyen (Ire) – Laurel Gift (Ire) (Presenting)

2018/19 b16g* b16g⁴ b16.3d³ May 1

A month on from winning historic back-to-back Grand Nationals with Tiger Roll in April, owner Michael O'Leary stunned the sport when announcing that he would be winding down his vast Gigginstown racing operation over the next five years. The forthright Ryanair chief executive made headlines in similar circumstances in 2016 when removing all his horses from Willie Mullins. Noel Meade was among the chief beneficiaries of that decision, enjoying 24 winners from 144 runners in the famous maroon silks in Ireland last season, and there should be plenty more to come, too, even if the Gigginstown name is to be seen less frequently in racecards.

These connections look to have an especially good prospect on their hands in the shape of Beacon Edge. He started out with Nicky Richards before being purchased privately after making a successful debut in an Ayr bumper last October, readily coming clear to win by four and a half lengths from a pair of subsequent winners. Beacon Edge's first start for Meade came in the Grade 2 bumper at the Dublin Racing Festival at Leopardstown in February, where he shaped well in finishing fourth in what proved to be a very strong event. He didn't get a clear run but was beaten only around three and a half lengths by the hugely-exciting Envoi Allen, who went on to glory in the big one at Cheltenham a month later.

Beacon Edge stepped up to Grade 1 company himself on his next outing in the Irish Champion Bumper at Punchestown and emerged as the best long-term prospect in a race that usually produces plenty of good jumpers. The front-running winner Colreevy wasn't for catching but Beacon Edge kept on well in his own right to take third near the finish (beaten a length and three quarters).

Beacon Edge is from a good National Hunt family; his dam is an unraced sister to the Grade 1-winning chaser Jessies Dream for Gordon Elliott, while his ill-fated half-brother Fridaynightlights was a big improver upon joining the same trainer, winning three handicap hurdles. His build suggests that his long-term future lies over fences, but, in the interim, he is very much the type to make his presence felt in some of the better novice hurdles in Ireland, with further than 2m likely to suit. *Noel Meade*

Conclusion: *Bumper winner for Nicky Richards who improved further when hitting the frame in a pair of graded events in the spring for new connections; smart prospect for novice hurdling*

Chacun Pour Soi (Fr)   c169p

7 b.g. Policy Maker (Ire) – Kruscyna (Fr) (Ultimately Lucky (Ire))
2018/19 c16d* c16d* May 2

Altior cemented his status as the top 2m chaser with another unbeaten campaign in 2018/19, but that title could be destined for the deeply exciting Chacun Pour Soi in the months ahead.

A juvenile hurdle winner on his debut in France in summer 2015, Chacun Pour Soi was purchased out of Emmanuel Clayeux's stable by Rich Ricci after a promising run on his first try over fences at Enghien the following spring. His new owner had to be patient, with Chacun Pour Soi subsequently off the track for three years, but he proved well worth the wait as he turned his comeback for Willie Mullins in a beginners chase at Naas in March into a procession. Backed off the boards under Paul Townend, Chacun Pour Soi never saw another horse as he made all in tremendous style, tanking through the race and jumping superbly.

Having run to an eye-catching Timeform rating of 152 on that occasion, Chacun Pour Soi was quickly parachuted into the deep waters of the Ryanair Novices' Chase at the Punchestown Festival in May, where he left no doubt that he's another star in the making for his top trainer. Again strong in the betting, despite the presence of

Chacun Pour Soi leads Defi du Seuil over the last at Punchestown

two Cheltenham Festival winners in opposition in the shape of Defi du Seuil and stablemate Duc des Genievres, Chacun Pour Soi coped easily with the big step up in class to run out an impressive winner once more, producing the kind of top-class performance rarely seen from a novice chaser as he pulled clear from a very strong field, ultimately winning by four and a quarter lengths with a bit in hand (going away at the finish).

Providing he stands more regular racing, Chacun Pour Soi can improve further upon his already-lofty Timeform rating of 169p, achieved after only three runs over fences, remember. He really has the world at his feet. *Willie Mullins*

Conclusion: *Won both starts over fences back from a long absence for Willie Mullins, destroying a field of proven Grade 1-performers at Punchestown on the latter occasion; remains open to more improvement and looks a hugely exciting prospect in the 2m division*

Dommage Pour Toi (Fr)   h140
6 b.g. Magadan (Ire) – Phenyl des Mottes (Fr) (Bonnet Rouge (Fr))
2018/19 h16.6d³ h20s² h20d* h20d⁵ May 3

The announcement that Michael O'Leary and the colours of his Gigginstown House Stud would be a less frequent sight on British and Irish racecourses in years to come—as covered in the previous write-up on Beacon Edge—hasn't prevented the owner and his all-conquering team from continuing to buy up-and-coming talent, and they were quick to move for the exciting Dommage Pour Toi after his gutsy success in a Grade 2 at Fairyhouse's Easter Festival. It's easy to see why.

Dommage Pour Toi has done nothing but progress in his four starts to date for Henry de Bromhead. Having been pulled up in a point at Rathcannon nine weeks earlier, hopes weren't too high for him ahead of his hurdling/stable debut in a maiden at Down Royal in January, but he belied his SP of 40/1 with a promising display to finish third behind Curious Times. He then went one place better in a similar event at Leopardstown in March, when he probably would have won had he jumped the last two hurdles better, just failing to catch The Red Menace after rallying.

Upped markedly in class, Dommage Pour Toi had just a couple below him in the betting for the Easter Festival Novices' Hurdle at Fairyhouse, but he marked himself down as a top prospect by following in the footsteps of Cheltenham Gold Cup winner Al Boum Photo and Cooldine with victory. Always prominent under Rachael Blackmore, he caught the eye throughout and dug deep to win by three quarters of a length from the equally promising Zero Ten.

Purchased privately by Gigginstown in the aftermath, Dommage Pour Toi produced an even better performance in form terms when fifth (beaten 10 lengths) on his final start in the Champion Novices' Hurdle at the Punchestown Festival, the effort of trying to give chase to *Fifty* member Reserve Tank taking its toll late on. Still relatively lightly raced, there are surely more races to be won with Dommage Pour Toi and he's very much one to look out for in novice events over the larger obstacles this term, with a switch to chasing—the job for which most Gigginstown recruits are destined—likely to be the making of him. **Henry de Bromhead**

Conclusion: *Came a long way in a short space of time over hurdles and should be in for another profitable season in novice chases at around 2½m–3m*

Envoi Allen (Fr)   b125

5 b.g. Muhtathir – Reaction (Fr) (Saint des Saints (Fr))
2018/19 b16g* b16d* b16g* b16.4s* Mar 13

All fans of National Hunt racing know only too well the vast array of talent Gordon Elliott has at his disposal, but the colours sported by his Champion Bumper winner Envoi Allen might have had some punters doing a double take and thinking they had turned up at Newmarket. Indeed, one of the more curious aspects during a typically eventful Cheltenham Festival was the sight of the famous Cheveley Park Stud colours appearing in the winners' enclosure, with the legendary Newmarket-based stud— and its owners Patricia and David Thompson—much more readily associated with high class Flat performers. Only this summer their Threat landed York's Gimcrack Stakes for Richard Hannon, while Veracious also took Newmarket's Falmouth Stakes for Sir Michael Stoute.

They are no strangers to success in the winter game, though, with Party Politics memorably winning the 1992 Grand National in Patricia Thompson's silks. And, now that they have committed to investing much more in jumps racing again, we can expect their famous red, white and blue colours to become a much more prominent fixture in the big races to come. Recent evidence is certainly positive in that regard— Envoi Allen wasn't the only Festival winner for them, with A Plus Tard also running out an impressive winner of the Close Brothers Novices' Handicap Chase on the opening day for Henry de Bromhead, while we shouldn't forget their much-vaunted bumper winner Malone Road, either, given how promising he looked before being sidelined due to a knee injury.

So, what of their Envoi Allen, acquired for £400,000 after an eye-catching maiden point win at Ballinaboola. Three impressive odds-on bumper wins quickly followed at Fairyhouse, Navan and Leopardstown before he lined up at Cheltenham, once more as favourite. And, in his biggest test of all, he didn't disappoint, again travelling

Envoi Allen looks an exciting prospect for novice hurdling

fluently before knuckling down well when challenged to win by three quarters of a length from the four-year-old Blue Sari, to whom he conceded 8 lb.

An imposing son of miler Muhtathir and out of a French staying chaser from the family of Auvergnat, Envoi Allen will have no problems staying 2½m, and it goes without saying that he is a most exciting prospect who is sure to take high rank amongst this season's novice hurdlers. *Gordon Elliott*

Conclusion: *Unbeaten Champion Bumper winner and most exciting prospect for novice hurdles*

Gardens of Babylon (Ire)   h141p
4 b.g. Camelot – Condition (Deploy)
2018/19 h16g* h16g² h16g² h16.8d³ h16d² h16d* :: 2019/20 h16.1g h16d Sep 10

Joseph O'Brien has made a seamless transition from top-flight rider to top-flight trainer, and one of the features of his fledgling training career thus far has been his propensity to deliver a surprise winner on the biggest of occasions, both on the Flat and over jumps. To name but a few, Rekindling (2017 Melbourne Cup at 14/1), Edwulf (2018 Irish Gold Cup at 33/1) and Latrobe (2018 Irish Derby at 14/1) have all plundered Group or Grade 1 prizes for their trainer at double-figure odds, and, in the shape of Gardens of Babylon, we think O'Brien could have another potential spoiler on his hands.

The 2019 Cheltenham Festival will be remembered for all the wrong reasons as far as O'Brien is concerned, with Sir Erec tragically losing his life in the Triumph Hurdle. Gardens of Babylon was the stable's second string in that race, and his fine staying-on third to Pentland Hills in first-time cheekpieces was understandably overshadowed by earlier events. Nevertheless, that run marked him down as a useful juvenile in his own right, and, not for the first time, it left us with the overriding impression that the son of Camelot was crying out for a step up in trip.

Even better efforts followed when kept to 2m for his next two starts, filling the runner-up spot in a Grade 2 at Fairyhouse before making the most of an easier opportunity in a novice at the Punchestown Festival, and there have been excuses for his defeats the last twice—he was unsuited by the steady gallop when making his handicap debut in the Galway Hurdle in early-August, while it was very much Groundhog Day with him when eighth in another handicap at Listowel the following month, once again doing his best work at the end of the 2m journey, a race in which he was tasked with attempting to concede 15 lb and upwards to 13 rivals.

We are happy to forgive Gardens of Babylon those efforts under the circumstances and remain of the strong opinion that he will come into his own and win some good races when granted the opportunity to tackle longer distances. He is certainly well worth another chance to prove himself better than a mark of 142 in handicaps, and, given his trainer's penchant for spoiling the party, it isn't beyond the realms of possibility that he could line up as an interesting outsider for the Stayers' Hurdle come the Cheltenham Festival. *Joseph O'Brien*

Conclusion: *Useful 2m novice with the potential to improve plenty once joining the staying division*

 Gypsy Island (Ire)   **b117**

5 b.m. Jeremy (USA) – Thieving Gypsy (Ire) (Presenting)
2018/19 b16.2d* h16d² b16d* b16d* b16.3d* May 1

It's not often a trainer is happy to see his stable star suffer defeat, but Peter Fahey was quick to count his blessings after Gypsy Island lost on her hurdling bow at Navan last November. Only narrowly denied by the useful Put The Kettle On that day, Fahey subsequently made the decision to build up the mare's experience in bumpers— preserving her novice status for the following year—and what a decision it proved to be.

Gypsy Island already had winning form in bumpers to her name, when impressively landing at gamble at Ballinrobe three months before her Navan reversal, and she quickly got back on the up on her return to that sphere in the spring, establishing herself amongst the best of her sex with ready wins at Naas in March and Fairyhouse in April, taking the step up to listed level in her stride on the latter occasion, full value on the day for the 11-length winning margin.

A further step up in class beckoned, and Gypsy Island didn't disappoint when lining up in a Grade 3 at the Punchestown Festival, ridden with supreme confidence off the pace before scything through the field to win hard held by five lengths. There's no doubting that she would have been well worth her place in the Grade 1 bumper at the same meeting—her earlier outing over hurdles made her ineligible for that race—and, by our reckoning, that Punchestown performance put her within 8 lb of Champion Bumper winner Envoi Allen, without factoring in her sex allowance once they go hurdling.

Given the aptitude that Gypsy Island has already demonstrated for that job, it goes without saying that she looks sure to rack up the wins in novice company, with the Dawn Run Mares' Novices' Hurdle at the Cheltenham Festival appealing as an obvious target at this early stage—she could well end up contesting the Supreme Novices' Hurdle such is her undoubted talent. Either way, Gypsy Island is one of the most exciting novices on either side of the Irish Sea, and we await her return with great interest. *Peter Fahey*

Conclusion: : *Exciting bumper mare who is one to follow in novice hurdles, with the Dawn Run at the Cheltenham Festival likely to feature highly on her agenda*

Honeysuckle   h140p

5 b.m. Sulamani (Ire) – First Royal (Ger) (Lando (Ger))
2018/19 h20g* h16g* h18s* h20g* Apr 21

Honeysuckle plants are known for their climbing qualities, and Henry de Bromhead's exciting mare can go down as aptly named if her rapid rise through the ranks in 2018/19 is anything to go by, with nothing able to get within three lengths of her in four novice hurdling starts against her own sex.

Picked up for €110,000 following an impressive point win, Honeysuckle offered the first indication that she might be able to justify that price tag with an effortless victory on her hurdling debut at Fairyhouse (2½m) last November, jumping/travelling fluently throughout the contest, before drawing clear in the straight to justify odds-on favouritism by 12 lengths. A listed win came just as easily to her at Thurles (2m) the following month, and, having extended her winning sequence to three in Grade 3 company back at Fairyhouse (2¼m) in January, it was no surprise that she featured prominently in the ante-post betting for the Dawn Run Mares' Novices' Hurdle at the Cheltenham Festival in the spring.

Unfortunately for her connections, Honeysuckle was ruled out of that race the week before the meeting, but it didn't take her long to bounce back from that setback

Honeysuckle extends her unbeaten record to four at Fairyhouse

and conclusively prove herself the best novice of her sex, with a first Grade 1 success coming her way in the Irish Stallion Farms EBF Mares' Novices' Hurdle Championship Final at Fairyhouse (2½m) on her final start. Half the field from the Dawn Run—the winner, third and fourth among them—took their chance at Fairyhouse, but all of them were ultimately powerless to resist Honeysuckle, who typically cruised through the race before bursting clear to beat a subsequent listed winner by five and a half lengths.

A tough and uncomplicated mare who is four from four under Rules, Honeysuckle has already achieved plenty for a mere five-year-old, and the most exciting part is that she is yet to be tested. Her point win suggests that her long-term future is likely to lie over fences, but, in the interim, she appeals as one who should continue to take all the beating in the mares' hurdling division, while it's to be hoped that she gets the chance to show her worth against geldings at some stage, too. **Henry de Bromhead**

Conclusion: *Unbeaten in four novice hurdling starts against her own sex and could be the one to break Willie Mullins' stranglehold on the Mares' Hurdle at the Cheltenham Festival with further improvement on the cards*

Its All Guesswork (Ire) c125p

7 b.g. Mahler – La Lambertine (Fr) (Glaieul (USA))
2018/19 c22.5d^3 c19.9g^2 c22s^2 c20g* c24g^F h24d^3 c26d Mar 14

Its All Guesswork laid some solid foundations as a novice chaser through the early part of the last campaign, finishing placed in some strong events at Galway, Kilbeggan and Listowel before making the most of a good opportunity to get off the mark at Navan last September, doing it easily having jumped fluently for the most part.

His jumping proved less dependable on his handicap debut in the Munster National at Limerick the following month—he fell at the last when likely to be placed—and instead it's what he did on the back of a mid-season break that identifies him as an interesting one for the future. Noticeably easy to back ahead of his return to hurdling in a competitive Pertemps qualifier at Punchestown in February, he caught the eye in no uncertain terms when staying on strongly from a long way back to finish third, a run that seemed likely to put him spot on for a tilt at a valuable handicap back over fences. The Kim Muir at the Cheltenham Festival proved to be target of choice, but, in the event, he wasn't seen to best effect, left with too much do and, more importantly, said to have returned lame.

Its All Guesswork hasn't been seen since, but this tall gelding remains with untapped potential as a chaser, particularly as he's totally unexposed over long distances. Gordon Elliott is as shrewd as it gets when it comes to targeting major handicap prizes and, in Its All Guesswork, he has a progressive staying chaser who's likely to be primed for one of the big early-season races—he has unfinished business with the Munster National and would be of interest if attempting to make amends from only 1 lb higher this time round, while the Troytown also appeals as a suitable target, a race Elliott has won on four occasions since 2014. *Gordon Elliott*

Conclusion: *Tall, chasing type who is yet to have a fair crack at handicap chases over 3m+ and could be in for a breakthrough season in 2019/20*

The Big Dog (Ire) h129p

6 b.g. Mahler – Saddlers Leader (Ire) (Saddlers' Hall (Ire))
2018/19 h24v^4 h20g^2 h20s* h22g h20d^2 May 1

A bumper winner back in January 2018, The Big Dog didn't pull up any trees as a novice hurdler last term, his sole success coming in a 17-runner maiden over 2½m at Gowran Park, staying on strongly to record his second Rules win a year on from his first. Plenty of winners came out of that race, and he signed off with an excellent effort of his own when second to the highly promising Zero Ten at the Punchestown Festival in May, but these exploits have only scratched the surface of his ability.

An ex-pointer by Mahler, this lightly-raced six-year-old has always looked the sort to come into his own as a staying chaser, and, bearing in mind that he's had just the one go over 3m under Rules—when pitched straight into a Grade 3 on his hurdling debut—there's every reason to expect a lot more from Peter Fahey's gelding in future. An immediate switch to the larger obstacles is expected, and he should be able to pick up a novice without much trouble before moving into a higher grade, where his uncomplicated style should stand him in good stead.

Although an exciting novice chasing prospect, The Big Dog is likely to prove more of a slow burner than the bulk of this year's *Fifty*, one to keep on the radar even into the following campaign, when he could be challenging for some of the top-end staying handicaps in Ireland. **Peter Fahey**

Conclusion: *Unexposed as a stayer and appeals as very much the sort to improve for a switch to chasing, with long-distance handicaps likely to be his ultimate destination*

SECTION

TALKING TO THE TRAINERS

We asked a number of leading National Hunt trainers to pick out a stable star, handicapper, and dark horse to follow for the coming season. Here's what they said...

Harry Fry

Wins-Runs in Britain in 2018/19	**47/242**
Highest-rated horse in training	**If The Cap Fits** Timeform Rating h159+

Star Performer: If The Cap Fits (h159+): "He relished the step up in trip to win the Grade 1 Ryanair Stayers Hurdle at Aintree in April. We are looking forward to another season hurdling that will be geared around the Stayers' Hurdle in March. He could reappear at either Wetherby or Ascot in November, which will hopefully lead onto the Long Walk Hurdle at Ascot before Christmas."

Handicapper: Just A Sting (c134): "He made a perfect start to his chasing career, winning his first two starts followed by a good second at Kempton over Christmas. Things didn't go to plan in the spring, but he can bounce back to form this autumn on decent ground, with something like the Sodexo Gold Cup at Ascot an early season target."

Dark Horse: Over To Sam (c131p): "He has spent a lot of time off the track, but ran with plenty of promise after such a long layoff on his chasing debut at Newton Abbot in May. He needs soft ground, but can make up for lost time this winter over fences."

Tom George

Wins-Runs in Britain in 2018/19	**52/377**
Highest-rated horse in training	**God's Own** Timeform Rating c159

Star Performer: Summerville Boy (h152): "He had a poor start to last season due to injury, but showed signs of a return to form at Punchestown in April, when he wasn't beaten far in the Champion Hurdle. He has schooled well over fences and should come into his own now chasing."

Handicapper: Doctor Dex (h122): "He won two hurdle races for us last season, despite still looking green, and there should be plenty of improvement to come from him in his novice chase campaign."

Dark Horse: Let's Go Champ (–): "He has an outstanding pedigree, being closely related to the Triumph Hurdle winner Our Conor. He was an impressive winner of his only point-to-point at Bartlemy in May and could develop into a very exciting sort under Rules."

Nicky Henderson

Wins-Runs in Britain in 2018/19	**141/544**
Highest-rated horse in training	**Altior** Timeform Rating c180p

Star Performer: Santini (c161p): "This is a difficult one as we are unaware of Altior's plan as yet, so I might suggest Santini. He could start in the 3m Graduation Chase at Sandown and then we'll see if he's up to races like the King George."

Handicapper: Valtor (c157+): "I think he is capable of progressing and may start at Ascot in November."

Dark Horse: Shishkin (b101p): "I thought Shishkin was impressive in his bumper and I think he will make a nice novice hurdler."

Philip Hobbs

Wins-Runs in Britain in 2018/19	**106/560**
Highest-rated horse in training	**Defi du Seuil** Timeform Rating c164p

Star Performer: Defi du Seuil (c164p): "He has been a superstar for us and is still only a six-year-old. He should be competitive in top condition chasers, but I am not sure over which trip yet."

Handicapper: Deise Aba (h121p): "I don't know if he will start in a handicap hurdle, but more likely a novice handicap chase over 3m off 135. He was inexperienced and nervous last season, but should improve."

Dark Horse: Truckers Pass (–): "We have been really pleased with him after his second on his only start in point-to-points. He had an ongoing cough, which has now hopefully disappeared after a summer at grass."

Alan King

Wins-Runs in Britain in 2018/19	**91/499**
Highest-rated horse in training	**Sceau Royal** Timeform Rating c164

Star Performer: Sceau Royal (c164): "The plan would be to start him off in the Shloer Chase at Cheltenham, a race he won last year. He could then go for the Tingle Creek at Sandown, unless the ground came up really heavy, in which case we may switch to the Peterborough at Huntingdon. All those conditions races at around two miles will come into consideration."

Handicapper: Giving Glances (h114): "She won a couple last season, including a listed race at Doncaster. She went slightly off the boil in the spring, but she probably was just over the top. She's had a good break and I'd like to think that she might just be better than her handicap mark [122]."

Dark Horse: Edwardstone (b101): "He finished second three times in bumpers last season. I think he bumped into a decent horse every time and the plan would be to go straight into novice hurdles with him."

Olly Murphy

Wins-Runs in Britain in 2018/19	**82/431**
Highest-rated horse in training	**Thomas Darby** Timeform Rating h147

Star Performer: Thomas Darby (h147): "Runner-up in last season's Supreme Novices' Hurdle, he has done fantastic for a break and will go novice chasing in the autumn. He will start over 2m and will hopefully turn out to be a very smart novice."

Handicapper: The Wolf (h115): "A new horse to the yard, he had some eye-catching novice form last season and could turn out to be well-handicapped on a mark of 124."

Dark Horse: Dundrum Wood (b92): "I was amazed he got beat when finishing second in his bumper last season. He shows plenty at home and could be a very smart novice hurdler; one to keep on the right side of."

Paul Nicholls

Wins-Runs in Britain in 2018/19	**135/589**
Highest-rated horse in training	**Cyrname** Timeform Rating c173+

Star Performer: Cyrname (c173+): "The plan with Cyrname is to go to Ascot at the end of November [for the 1965 Chase) and then will have an entry in the King George."

Handicapper: Dolos (c158): "Dolos is a smart young horse who we plan to start off in the Haldon Gold Cup at Exeter in November. He will then run in all the top handicaps."

Dark Horse: Cap du Mathan (h109p): "A lovely young horse who had two runs in Auteuil last year, finishing fourth on his debut and then second on his next start. He looks sure to win a maiden hurdle and progress."

Cyrname looks set for another productive campaign

Jonjo O'Neill

Wins-Runs in Britain in 2018/19 **56/472**

Highest-rated horse in training **Champagne At Tara** Timeform Rating c140§

Star Performer: Django Django (h130): "We kept Django Django over the smaller obstacles last season and it culminated in him winning the valuable Stayers' Final at Haydock. That race had been his target and it worked out well. I feel he is still unexposed granted a test of stamina and we will look to start him off in a handicap hurdle in October before heading over fences, where I'm hoping we will see a proper horse."

Handicapper: Cloth Cap (c135p): "We sent him chasing last season and he improved as we hoped he would. He ran a superb race for a horse with such little experience when third on his final start in the Scottish National. I'm hoping there is some mileage in his current mark and I will be targeting some of the seasons bigger handicaps. Trevor loves having Grand National runners and Aintree will be the long-term plan."

Dark Horse: On The Bandwagon (–): "We loved this horse at the Aintree sales and were delighted to secure him. By Oscar and from the family of the top class Nick Dundee and Ned Kelly, he came second on his only start in Irish points-to-points at Monksgrange, staying on really nicely. A big, strong sort, he will start in a bumper before going novice hurdling."

David Pipe

Wins-Runs in Britain in 2018/19	**44/363**
Highest-rated horse in training	**Ramses de Teillee** Timeform Rating c152

Star Performer: Eden du Houx (b112): "He was impressive in two bumpers last season and has strengthened up well during the summer. He will be going over hurdles this season."

Handicapper: Remastered (h127): "He performed well last season and probably ran his best race in defeat behind Drashel Dasher at Newbury. He loves soft ground and hopefully there will be more to come from him this season. A step up to 3m should also suit."

Dark Horse: Jasmin des Bordes (h114p): "He ran well in his bumper and on his first start over hurdles. He has had a wind operation during the summer and should be seen to better effect this term with his novice status still intact."

Dan Skelton

Wins-Runs in Britain in 2018/19	**205/988**
Highest-rated horse in training	**Ch'tibello** Timeform Rating h155

Star Performer: Roksana (h149): "She was a first Grade 1 winner for both Harry and myself when winning the Mares' Hurdle at the Cheltenham Festival and very nearly followed up in the Liverpool Hurdle on Grand National day, only being beaten a head by If The Cap Fits. We would hope she can continue to progress this season and mix it with the boys at the top level."

Handicapper: Spiritofthegames (c150): "A tough and consistent performer who has been banging on the door in big handicaps over both hurdles and fences. He started off last season with victory in a listed novices' chase at Chepstow and ran very well to finish on the podium at the Cheltenham Festival in the Brown Advisory & Merribelle Stable Plate. We feel he has unfinished business in handicaps and hope he can pick up a big one this season."

Dark Horse: Generation Text (–): "He was purchased from Denis Murphy at the Cheltenham Festival Sale having finished second in a strong Irish point-to-point on his only start. He has been showing up nicely at home in his early work and we would hope he can figure highly in novice hurdles this season."

RISING STARS

Christian Williams

Base	**Ogmore-by-Sea, South Glamorgan**
First Full Licence	**2017**
First Jumps Winner	**Juge Et Parti** Bangor 22/04/2017
Total Winners	**44**
Best Horse Trained	**Potters Corner** Timeform Rating c140

Christian Williams' career in the saddle was punctuated by some serious injuries—including breaking both arms in a fall at Cheltenham—but it also brought him 339 wins, including victories on some household names in the sport. A large proportion of those successes came for Paul Nicholls, among them three novice hurdles in the early career of future Gold Cup winner Denman, while Williams also finished second in a Grand National on Royal Auclair for the same stable. Williams' last rides were in the spring of 2013, but it was to be another four years before he took out his own training licence. In the interim, he assisted with the pre-training of the young horses belonging to leading owner Dai Walters. It was from Walters' stables near Cardiff that Williams sent out his first winner, Juge Et Parti, who carried the owner's dark blue and white diabolo colours to success in a bumper at Bangor in April 2017. However, less than a year later Williams moved to his own yard at the family farm on the South Wales coast to train in partnership with his brother Nicky, himself a successful rider in points. In his first full season at his new base, Williams sent out 27 winners, with the highlight being the 20/1-success of Potters Corner in the Midlands Grand National at Uttoxeter. With eight winners on the board already in the current season at the time of writing—three of those courtesy of the five-year-old Game Line, who has won over both hurdles and fences—there's every chance of that total being beaten this term. Surprisingly, Williams has yet to have a winner at Chepstow (something Potters Corner will surely attempt to put right in the Welsh National) and has registered only one win at his other local track Ffos Las, but it's been a different story when the yard's runners have made the trek to Norfolk, with an impressive 10 wins from 30 runners at Fakenham.

Emmet Mullins

Base	**Closutton, County Carlow**
First Full Licence	**2015**
First Jumps Winner	**St Stephens Green** Kilbeggan 22/06/2015
Total Winners	**29**
Best Horse Trained	**Zero Ten** Timeform Rating c/h138p

Emmet Mullins made the perfect start to his training career in 2015 when his very first runner, St Stephens Green, was backed off the boards before his success in a bumper at Kilbeggan. That initial win was very much a family affair, as St Stephens Green had made a promising debut for the trainer's uncle Willie on his only previous start, and he had the assistance of another champion from the Mullins clan, cousin Patrick, in the saddle. Like Patrick and Willie, Emmet Mullins had himself enjoyed success as a jockey at the Cheltenham Festival, winning the 2011 Martin Pipe Conditional Jockeys' Handicap Hurdle on Sir des Champs, trained by his uncle, while another highlight of his riding career was a Grade 3 novices' hurdle win at Limerick aboard future Champion Hurdle winner Faugheen. Since that Kilbeggan win, further success has followed under both codes for Emmet Mullins as a trainer, with the last 12 months proving particularly productive. Highlights have included wins at both the Punchestown and Galway Festivals for the stable's best jumper Zero Ten (his successful chasing debut at Galway was one of three winners for the yard at that meeting), while bumper winner Sneaky Getaway has developed into a useful stayer on the Flat. The latter's Doncaster Cup challenge ultimately proved unsuccessful, but Mullins' success has not been confined to Ireland, as the mare Yeats Baby twice landed gambles from a total of three victories in handicap hurdles in Britain last season, while Mullins took a leaf out of his uncle Willie's book by winning a listed hurdle for three-year-old fillies at Auteuil in September with Fujimoto Flyer. Further evidence of Emmet Mullins sharing the family trait of seeking out international opportunities came when he sent Tornado Watch across the Atlantic to finish second in last season's Grand National Hurdle at Far Hills, New Jersey.

Darragh O'Keeffe

Attached Stable	**Enda Bolger**
First Ride	**2017**
First Winner	**William du Berlais** Killarney 17/07/2018
Total Winners	**52**
Best Jumps Horse Ridden	**Ballyoisin** Timeform Rating c166

'A young Mallow man started pony racing earlier this year and since then he has gone from strength to strength as a genuine and true contender for the future as a jockey in the top grade.' Rewind the clock to December 2010 and 10-year-old Darragh O'Keeffe had already been identified as a huge talent in the saddle by writers at the Irish Independent. It was more than six years after that article was written before O'Keeffe had his first ride under Rules, when partnering Strategic Heights to sixth in a Dundalk handicap in March 2017, but he has attracted plenty more headlines in the short time since, with the turning point coming when he switched his attentions to the National Hunt game and linked up with Enda Bolger. A first success in that sphere came courtesy of William du Berlais at Killarney in July 2018—the same horse provided him with his second win at Tipperary just five days later—while the second half of 2018 taught O'Keeffe an early lesson about the ups and downs associated with being a jump jockey; having partnered the Bolger-trained Ballyoisin to a landmark victory in a valuable handicap hurdle at Listowel in September, he was then ruled out of action for the rest of the year after fracturing his wrist in a fall at Gowran Park 23 days later. Back in the saddle in late-January, O'Keeffe ended his first full season with 14 winners, while he very nearly brought the house down when guiding former Champion Hurdle hero Jezki to a narrow defeat in the Ladbrokes Hurdle at Leopardstown's Dublin Racing Festival. As much promise as he demonstrated last term, though, few could have expected how well O'Keeffe has started the current campaign, with 39 winners—including three at the Galway Festival—already on the board at this relatively early stage of proceedings. To put his achievements into context, that figure puts him only three behind 2018/19 winner Paul Townend in the jockeys' championship at the time of writing, while he is 19 clear of his nearest rival in the race to be crowned champion conditional and all but guaranteed to surpass the tallies recorded by Jack Kennedy (45 winners in 2016) and Jonathan Burke (42 in 2015), the only other conditionals since 2000 to have ridden more than 40 winners in a season. Put simply, Darragh O'Keeffe is a rising star in every sense of the world and one who is destined for the 'top grade' of jockeys, if not there already.

Connor Brace

Attached Stable	**Fergal O'Brien**
First Ride	**2018**
First Winner	**Billygwyn Too** Exeter 24/04/2018
Total Winners	**37**
Best Jumps Horse Ridden	**Verdana Blue** Timeform Rating h159

Born in Wales, it was nonetheless in Scotland that Connor Brace landed the biggest win of his fledgling career to date, when partnering Verdana Blue to an impressive success in the Scottish Champion Hurdle at Ayr in April. With the Christmas Hurdle winner set to carry top weight of 11-10, Brace took a valuable 7 lb off the mare's back, and it spoke volumes for the excellent impression he'd made in less than 12 months since riding his very first winner under Rules in an Exeter bumper for amateur riders the previous spring that Nicky Henderson entrusted the ride to the then 17-year-old. While it's still early days in Brace's professional career, he has a good few years of experience in the saddle, progressing from pony racing to the Welsh pointing circuit in which his grandfather David is a leading figure. Brace's first win in points came at the age of just 16, and the same season he won the National Novice Riders' Championship in that sphere, following in the footsteps of another Welsh teenager to have since made his mark as a professional jockey, James Bowen. Brace also spent time working for Philip Hobbs, another top trainer who has supplied him with winning rides. However, it was the Cotswold yard of Fergal O'Brien which Brace joined once turning conditional in the autumn of 2018 and which will be making best use of the rider's claim—now down to 5 lb—in the months ahead. Brace has already notched up more than a dozen wins for his attached stable, including a double at Perth in April. That was the third time the rider had completed a 'brace' of winners during the 2018/19 season, and it was a feat that he accomplished again on a couple of horses trained by his grandfather at Worcester in July. That came just before Brace sprung a 25/1-surprise on Grapevine in the valuable Summer Handicap Hurdle at Market Rasen for trainer Sophie Leech.

ANTE-POST BETTING

Timeform's Features Writer John Ingles takes a look at the markets for some of the highlights in the National Hunt calendar and picks out his best value bets...

'New Beast from the East to hit UK during 'coldest winter in 30 years''. At least, that was one newspaper's take on recent research by a team of climate experts predicting the return, in the early months of 2020, of the sub-zero conditions which, among other things, resulted in six consecutive days without any jumping in Britain or Ireland in the run-up to the Cheltenham Festival a couple of seasons ago. It wouldn't have sold as many papers, of course, but the slightly less alarming truth behind the headline—if the scientists are correct—is that we can apparently expect *'the coldest winter since January-February 2013'* and *'the 23rd coldest winter since 1953'*. As for the Met Office, they're keeping an open mind. *'We believe it is way too early to say what is going to happen in the winter months,'* said their spokesman. *'Even forecasting events for a couple of weeks can be a bit of a challenge. We generally concentrate on the next five days, which we are really good at.'* Wise words from the weathermen. Now who else would be foolish enough to try to predict events months in advance?

King George VI Chase

Paul Nicholls won Kempton's Boxing Day highlight for the tenth time when **Clan des Obeaux** beat former winner **Thistlecrack** and the then reigning Gold Cup winner **Native River** in last season's King George. That's top-class form and, still only seven, there's every reason to think Clan des Obeaux will be primed for a defence of his title. In fact, all three of Nicholls' past King George winners, See More Business, Kauto Star and Silviniaco Conti came back to win it again—or again and again (five times in all) in Kauto's Star's case—he too a six-year-old when he won it for the first time. But Clan des Obeaux won't have things all his own way. There's the likelihood of at least one top-class rival stepping up in trip, as well as a talented crop of last season's novices to contend with. Potentially the most fascinating aspect of this season's King George is the prospect of **Altior** (3/1 favourite with most firms at the time of writing) putting his unbeaten record over jumps on the line on a first try at 3m. We should have a clearer idea of his stamina by then if he tackles the 1965 Chase over an intermediate trip at

La Bague Au Roi (left) and Topofthegame jump the last together in the Kauto Star

Ascot beforehand. That race could also feature Altior's long-awaited clash with Clan des Obeaux's stablemate **Cyrname**, twice an impressive winner over the same C&D last term, though he too would be going into unknown territory distance-wise in the King George. **Lostintranslation**, who would be bidding to give Colin Tizzard a third King George in five years, heads the second-season chasers in the ante-post betting, though it's worth pointing out that he was twice beaten last season by the hugely likeable **La Bague Au Roi**. Warren Greatrex's mare also won a cracking renewal of the Kauto Star Novices' Chase last Boxing Day (she has won both of her starts at Kempton) from Topofthegame and **Santini**, and met with her only defeat over fences to date over an inadequate trip at Aintree. Back at 3m, there's likely to be more to come from her and she looks a value each-way bet at this stage.

SELECTION: **La Bague Au Roi (16/1 each-way)**

Champion Hurdle

The freak accident at home over the summer that ultimately claimed the life of the Champion Hurdle winner Espoir d'Allen leaves the ante-post market for next year's race rather threadbare. Willie Mullins and Nicky Henderson look to be holding all the aces, and Mullins has the current favourite (at no bigger than 7/2) **Klassical Dream**. It's been a very long time since a Supreme Novices' winner has won the Champion Hurdle 12 months later, but Klassical Dream went on to take his unbeaten record for Mullins to four when following up every bit as emphatically at Punchestown. Even so, former dual Champion Hurdle winner **Buveur d'Air** is the top two-miler as things stand, and while he suffered some reverses last term (notably the fall which ended his hopes of winning for a third time at Cheltenham), his return to winning ways at Punchestown, avenging an Aintree defeat at the hands of **Supasundae**, was a reminder that he's still very much one to reckon with on the Champion Hurdle scene. However, Nicky Henderson also had two of last season's leading juvenile hurdlers, and while unbeaten Triumph Hurdle winner **Pentland Hills** is the shorter of that pair in the betting, **Fusil Raffles** gave a bigger beating to **Fakir d'Oudairies** at Punchestown than Pentland Hills did when following up his Triumph success at Aintree. Espoir d'Allen showed that the jump can be made from juvenile hurdler to Champion Hurdle winner in the space of 12 months, but he was the first to manage it since Katchit in 2008. Besides the current favourite, Mullins has other possible contenders, including last season's dual Grade 1 winner **Sharjah** who was brought down by Buveur d'Air's fall in March. But Sharjah's owners Susannah and Rich Ricci also have **Saldier** who never got the chance last term to build on a promising juvenile campaign. His last win as a four-year-old came at Punchestown where he beat stablemate **Mr Adjudicator** who has gone on to better things since. Saldier looked all set to make a winning reappearance in a Grade 3 contest at Naas last November only to fall at the last. Who was left clear to win? Espoir d'Allen. Saldier wasn't seen out again, but he's got the potential to strengthen his Champion Hurdle claims when he gets back to the track this term.

SELECTION: Saldier (20/1 each-way)

Queen Mother Champion Chase

Whatever **Altior** does in the King George, we don't see him as a Gold Cup horse, while the Ryanair is unlikely to have enough pulling power to tempt him away from his only other Cheltenham Festival option, a bid for a third Champion Chase. On that basis, current odds as big as 4/1 are pretty tempting for a race he has previously won at even-money and 11/4-on. On the other hand, Altior can expect to face a stronger challenge in a potential hat-trick bid than he did when beating **Politologue** and **Sceau Royal**, after both gave him a scare, last March. In fact, Willie Mullins could probably run a good private version of his own Champion Chase at home if he wanted. **Min**, although beaten by **Un de Sceaux** at Punchestown, is probably the pick of the established 2m chasers at Closutton, though he has finished behind Altior in the last two renewals, while **Footpad** would need to recapture his impressive novice form and **Douvan** missed all of last season. From last year's novice ranks, **Chacun Pour Soi** is as exciting

Le Richebourg was ruled out of the major spring festivals through injury

a prospect as any of those were in their younger days after having his Arkle-winning stablemate **Duc des Genievres** a long way back in third at Punchestown (the JLT winner **Defi du Seuil** was runner-up). But Chacun Pour Soi's rare appearances to date mean that anyone getting involved at single-figure odds at this stage might also want to send some cotton wool Mullins' way just in case. Also in the '*talented but fragile*' category is **Cilaos Emery**, who had Duc des Genievres back in third when winning his only start over fences to date at Gowran. Cilaos Emery was just one of several absentees from the latest Arkle, and another important one was **Le Richebourg** who had been ante-post favourite for the race until Joseph O'Brien had to rule him out following an injury. Prior to that, Le Richebourg had only been beaten once in five starts over fences (by the high-class Delta Work over 2½m), looking a hugely exciting novice and impressing in particular with his jumping. The Queen Mother Champion Chase is a race the Festival's most successful owner J. P. McManus has never won, but perhaps Le Richebourg can put that right.

SELECTION: Le Richebourg (20/1 each-way)

Cheltenham Gold Cup

Can he do it again? Willie Mullins had a long wait to win his first Gold Cup in 2019 and starts the season with the first two in the betting for 2020. It was **Al Boum Photo** who broke his trainer's duck in the Festival's main event, but he's only second favourite behind stablemate **Kemboy** to become the first since Best Mate to defend his Gold Cup crown successfully. Kemboy was the shortest-priced of Mullins' four runners in the latest Gold Cup only to unseat at the first, but there were no jumping blemishes in his impressive beating of King George winner **Clan des Obeaux** (who didn't get home in the Gold Cup) at Aintree next time, and he made it six wins from his last six completed starts when battling to a two-length victory over Al Boum Photo in the Punchestown Gold Cup. Kemboy is one of only two horses to have beaten Al Boum Photo over fences to date and they are worthy holders of their places at the head of the betting. Thorough stayers **Native River** and **Anibale Fly**, first and third in 2018, both made the frame again in March despite less testing conditions, but that's probably the best they can aspire to in another attempt. **Presenting Percy**, who started favourite for the latest Gold Cup despite a less than ideal preparation, finished lame but makes most appeal of the beaten horses if taking his chance again. **Tiger Roll** would certainly be well worth his place in a Gold Cup but his chances of lining up would seem slim, popular though he'd be. Instead, it's last season's novices who look best placed to challenge Mullins' big two. Little more than two lengths covered the trio of Topofthegame, **Santini** and **Delta Work** who finished clear in the RSA Chase at Cheltenham, and though the former is now on the sidelines due to injury, the pair who chased him home both have Gold Cup potential. Delta Work underlined that by winning with plenty in hand at Punchestown next time, while another second-season

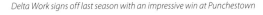

Delta Work signs off last season with an impressive win at Punchestown

chaser to consider is JLT runner-up **Lostintranslation**, the horse who went on to beat Topofthegame so impressively in the Mildmay Novices' Chase at Aintree and remains unexposed over beyond 3m. There's a good case for having two shots at the Gold Cup, therefore, and we'll go with one on each side of the Irish Sea.

SELECTION: **Delta Work and Lostintranslation (both 14/1)**

Grand National

Not even Red Rum could win three Grand Nationals in a row. He managed to win a third one, eventually, of course, but having carried 12-0 to victory for his second win, he was unable to concede 11 lb to former Gold Cup winner L'Escargot under the same burden in his hat-trick bid in 1975. The top weight in the Grand National is 11-10 these days but, even so, whether **Tiger Roll**, winner of the last two Grand Nationals, goes for the treble at all remains to be seen. Among mixed messages from connections, his trainer Gordon Elliott sounds a lot more positive about Tiger Roll taking his chance, but, either way, we're happy to look beyond the 6/1 favourite at this stage and there are plenty to choose from! **Talkischeap**, one of our *Fifty*, makes plenty of appeal given the way he ended his novice season over fences for Alan King by running away with the bet365 Gold Cup at Sandown, jumping superbly and then quickening clear to win by 10 lengths in a manner not readily associated with staying chasers. Another *Fifty* member is **Cloth Cap**, he too a seven-year-old who ended his novice season with a career-best effort in a major staying handicap in the spring. A staying-on third to Takingrisks in the Scottish Grand National, the Jonjo O'Neill-trained Cloth Cap would need to climb some more in the weights to get into the Grand National field, but after just four starts over fences—he's won two of them—that's entirely likely. Despite that lack of experience, he's a sound jumper, while his owner Trevor Hemmings has already won the Grand National three times. Ted Walsh is no stranger to winning the race, either, successful as a trainer with Papillon in 2000 and more recently saddling the 2012 third Seabass. Walsh has another likely type for the race in **Any Second Now**, who fell in the Irish Grand National when last seen but prior to that had relished the longest trip he'd tackled at that stage when staying on to win the Fulke Walwyn Kim Muir for amateur riders at the Cheltenham Festival.

SELECTION: **Talkischeap (33/1) and Cloth Cap (66/1)**

LEADING JUMPS SIRES

Still covering mares at the age of 27, **Flemensfirth** was crowned the leading jumps sire in Britain and Ireland (by prize money won) for the second season in succession in 2018/19, with the most sizeable contribution coming courtesy of Grand National runner-up Magic of Light. That was a performance with real historical weight as she became a rare mare to hit the frame at Aintree, matching Tiberetta's exploits in 1958 by finding only one too good, and, on that evidence, there are graded races to be won with her this season in receipt of her sex allowance. She wasn't the only talented mare to represent Flemensfirth on the track last term, either, with *Fifty* members Molly The Dolly and Queenohearts both gaining some valuable black type; there is likely to be more where that came from if they progress as expected in 2019/20.

As for the boys, Lostintranslation features prominently in the ante-post betting for the Cheltenham Gold Cup, a race that another of Flemensfirth's progeny, Imperial Commander, won in 2010. Lostintranslation won two of his six starts as a novice chaser last season, performing to a consistently high level, and is included in this year's *Fifty* as potentially a leading player for the blue riband, having dispatched paternal half-brother Topofthegame in impressive fashion when stepped up to three miles for his final start at Aintree. Along with Waiting Patiently, who is better than he was able to show in three starts last term, Lostintranslation is likely have some of the most valuable races of the season on his agenda, providing Flemensfirth with a very strong hand as he attempts to cement his status as the leading jumps sire in the business.

Sadler's Wells is best known for his exploits as a sire on the Flat, but his influence in National Hunt racing is also a significant one, as he demonstrated at the Cheltenham Festival—he was the paternal grandsire of nine winners at the meeting through his sons **Oscar** (Any Second Now and Paisley Park), **Milan** (Hazel Hill), **High Chaparral** (Altior), **Saddler Maker** (Eglantine du Seuil), **King's Theatre** (William Henry), **Beat Hollow** (Minella Indo), **Dream Well** (Klassical Dream) and **Court Cave** (City Island).

Oscar and Milan were second and third, respectively, amongst the season's leading sires. Lake View Lad won a couple of valuable handicap chases in the north for the former, but it was Paisley Park who emerged as comfortably his leading money earner, having completed a remarkable five-timer in the Stayers' Hurdle at Cheltenham. He is as short as 9/4 with some bookmakers to repeat those heroics at next year's Festival, while it could be a son of Milan who emerges as the chief pretender to his crown in the shape of If The Cap Fits; he produced a career best when winning the Liverpool Hurdle at Aintree on his final start, and, still totally unexposed as a stayer, it would be no surprise if had even more to offer this term. Other progeny of Milan to look out for include *Fifty* member McFabulous, who showed plenty of ability in winning three of his four starts in bumpers, and RSA runner-up Santini, who is another likely to be fighting it out for top honours as a staying chaser.

King's Theatre was crowned leading jumps sire for the fifth time in 2016/17, and while his death in 2011 will make it increasingly difficult for him to ever land a sixth title, his progeny have still done him proud in the last two seasons, carrying him to top-five finishes both times. William Henry provided him with yet another Cheltenham Festival winner when landing the latest renewal of the Coral Cup, and it could very easily have been two with only City Island denying the hitherto unbeaten Champ in the Ballymore. That was Champ's only defeat in six starts in novice hurdles during the latest campaign, and with further improvement on the cards, he has all the makings of a very smart chaser for his powerful connections in 2019/20.

Beneficial and **Presenting** are other now-deceased stallions who have regularly featured in the top few positions in recent years. The latter filled the runner-up spot behind King's Theatre for three consecutive seasons up to 2016/17 and enjoyed another solid campaign this time round, with Ballyoisin (Fortria Chase), Off You Go (Ladbrokes Hurdle) and Snow Falcon (Kerry National) doing most for the cause with big wins in Ireland. Meanwhile, Beneficial's progeny pocketed the best part of £2 million during the latest campaign, with Lady Buttons, who mixed chasing and hurdling to good effect all season, and Supreme runner-up Thomas Darby amongst those who helped to keep his name in the headlines. With a bit of luck, it should be more of the same for Beneficial in 2019/20, too, with Cloth Cap and Top Ville Ben both nominated in this year's *Fifty* as horses with the potential to make their presence felt in some of the season's most prestigious staying handicap chases.

Veteran chaser Wakanda knows all about doing that, and his victory in the Peter Marsh at Haydock last January helped to maintain **Westerner**'s position in the upper echelon of jumps sires, while Sue Smith also trained the top-rated progeny of **Midnight Legend** during the latest season in the shape of Relkeel Hurdle winner Midnight Shadow. Crosspark (Eider Chase) and Warriors Tale (Grand Sefton) also won big handicaps for Midnight Legend, while a dark horse for him this term could be Sky Pirate, who remains a maiden after five starts over fences to date but has been included in the *Fifty* as a result of the promise he showed when seventh in the Kim Muir at Cheltenham.

The other big winners at Cheltenham were provided by two French-based sires whose influence on these shores seems to be growing by the year. The ill-fated Champion Hurdle winner Espoir d'Allen was by **Voix du Nord**, who shot to prominence as the sire of Festival winners Taquin du Seuil and Vroum Vroum Mag earlier this decade. It's disappointing that Espoir d'Allen won't be around to further his legacy in years to come, but Voix du Nord still won't lack for top-class representation on the racecourse, with Defi du Seuil and Kemboy both looking likely contenders for big-race success once again in 2019/20—the former capped a fine first season over fences with victory in the JLT, while Kemboy ended the campaign as Timeform's top-rated staying chaser in training.

Kemboy cemented his status as the leader of his division when landing the Punchestown Gold Cup on his final start, winning by two lengths from stablemate Al Boum Photo. Their previous encounter in the Cheltenham Gold Cup had gone much less smoothly for Kemboy—he unseated jockey David Mullins at the first fence—and it was ultimately Al Boum Photo who did best of his yard's four runners to provide Willie Mullins with a first success in the blue riband, in the process becoming a second Festival winner for his sire **Buck's Boum**, following on from the Arkle success of another stablemate, Duc des Genievres, three days earlier. A full brother to the great staying hurdler Big Buck's, Buck's Boum's services are likely to have been in high demand during the 2019 breeding season, with another fine advert for the stallion coming in the shape of Dynamite Dollars, a Grade 1-winning novice chaser who was ruled out of the major spring festivals through injury.

Another stallion who has come a long way in a relatively short space of time is **Getaway**. Like Buck's Boum, he was only represented by his first runners in Britain and Ireland in 2015/16, since when the likes of Talkischeap (bet365 Gold Cup) and Verdana Blue (Christmas Hurdle/Scottish Champion Hurdle) have demonstrated his prowess as a sire with big-race wins, one in staying chases and the other in top-level hurdles over two miles. Clearly, he is well capable of throwing up different types, and one of his to look out for this season is the Paul Nicholls-trained Getaway Trump, who should take high rank in the novice chasing ranks following a progressive first campaign over the smaller obstacles.

Kayf Tara has been at this game much longer, but he enjoyed a slightly disappointing season by his usual very high standards in 2018/19, with the highlight coming courtesy of a narrow miss behind Clan des Obeaux (by **Kapgarde**) in the King George for Thistlecrack, a flagbearer for his sire in years gone by. Meanwhile, Darley may not appreciate it given that he is marketed as a Flat stallion, but a special mention must also go to **Authorized**, who joined a select group to have sired a chaser who has won more than one Grand National, with Tiger Roll—a Darley cast-off himself—once again defying his diminutive stature to add another chapter to his remarkable story at Aintree.

BET BETTER

SMART STATS LIVE

Get the standout strike rates, best bets and market movers

Add live results, news and tips with Smart Stats Live

Every race, every meeting every day

Only at timeform.com

SECTION

TIMEFORM'S VIEW

Chosen from the Timeform Formbook, here is Timeform's detailed analysis—compiled by our team of race reporters and supplemented by observations from Timeform's handicappers—of a selection of key races from the Cheltenham and Aintree festivals last spring.

CHELTENHAM Tuesday March 12
SOFT

Sky Bet Supreme Novices' Hurdle (Grade 1) (1)

Pos	Btn	Horse	Age	Wgt	Eq	Trainer	Jockey	SP
1		KLASSICAL DREAM (FR)	5	11-7		W. P. Mullins, Ireland	R. Walsh	6/1
2	4½	THOMAS DARBY (IRE)	6	11-7		Olly Murphy	Richard Johnson	28/1
3	½	ITCHY FEET (FR)	5	11-7		Olly Murphy	Gavin Sheehan	25/1
4	6	FAKIR D'OUDAIRIES (FR)	4	10-13		Joseph Patrick O'Brien, Ireland	J. J. Slevin	9/2jf
5	ns	FELIX DESJY (FR)	6	11-7		Gordon Elliott, Ireland	Sean Flanagan	11/1
6	hd	ARAMON (GER)	6	11-7		W. P. Mullins, Ireland	P. Townend	8/1
7	11	ANGELS BREATH (IRE)	5	11-7		Nicky Henderson	Nico de Boinville	6/1
8	1¼	MISTER FISHER (IRE)	5	11-7		Nicky Henderson	James Bowen	14/1
9	5	VISION D'HONNEUR (FR)	5	11-7	(t)	Gordon Elliott, Ireland	J. W. Kennedy	12/1
10	5	AL DANCER (FR)	6	11-7		Nigel Twiston-Davies	Sam Twiston-Davies	9/2jf
11	1½	GRAND SANCY (FR)	5	11-7	(h)	Paul Nicholls	Harry Cobden	14/1
12	8	THE BIG BITE (IRE)	6	11-7		Tom George	Noel Fehily	25/1
13	6	THE FLYING SOFA (FR)	6	11-7		Gary Moore	Jamie Moore	125/1
pu		BEAUFORT WEST (IRE)	5	11-7		Colin Tizzard	Robbie Power	66/1
pu		BRANDON CASTLE	7	11-7	(h+t)	Neil King	Bryony Frost	25/1
pu		NORMAL NORMAN	5	11-7		John Ryan	Paddy Brennan	100/1

16 ran Race Time 4m 00.10 Closing Sectional (4.10f): 59.1s (101.6%) Winning Owner: Mrs J Coleman

An unusually open renewal of the Supreme, with no one candidate having established themselves as the leader of the generation, the main trial races, mostly run on unseasonable ground, failing to throw up an obvious favourite, none of the field having achieved form good enough to win even an average recent running of the race; the winner found the improvement to think it was at least that, though the race as a whole set the pattern for the day with plenty of the other fancied contenders failing to give their running; it race saw the introduction of official times for jumps racing, at the moment just for the Festival, a development that should have happened years ago and which will hopefully be extended to all meetings in the not-too-distant future; the race was the first of 3 on the card for which there was a false start, but no blame was apportioned in any case. **Klassical Dream** kept to 2m, though the Baring Bingham was reportedly a serious option, maintained his unbeaten record since joining Willie Mullins, clearly very smart and looking to have a bright future, most likely as a chaser next season, his physique and demeanour both suggesting one that will come even more into his own over fences; prominent, jumped well, took keen hold, pressed leader from third, led on bridle soon after fifth, shaken up approaching last, kept on well, ridden out. **Thomas Darby** progressed again up in grade, still a bit raw but coping well with this class of opposition; held up, travelled well, mistake fourth, still plenty to do after next, good progress before 2 out, ridden straight, kept on well run-in, no match for winner; he was reportedly lame, but hopefully it won't be a longer-term problem and he has the makings of a smashing novice chaser for next season. **Itchy Feet** after 4 months off, ran well upped in grade, even if he was well served by the run of the race; held up, still plenty to do before 2 out, headway entering straight, hung left, mistake last, stayed on, reportedly bled; hopefully the physical problem won't prove a long-term concern, as he has a bright future, particularly over fences. **Fakir d'Oudairies** running here in preference to the Triumph, wants more of a test of stamina than this provided; chased leader, lost place 3 out, kept on well approaching last, took fourth close home; will be suited by further than 2m; remains with potential. **Felix Desjy** backed at long odds, ran up to his form last time, just not quite up to this task; mid-division, headway before fifth, every chance 2 out, no extra last; he needs to fill out still, but presumably will be chasing next season. **Aramon** wasn't disgraced, though he had virtually the same chance as the winner on their running last time; held up, not fluent 3 out, headway 2 out, chased leader entering straight, no extra last; he was having his fourth run in a Grade 1 novice and his merit seems well established. **Angels Breath** failed to meet expectations, possibly finding this coming sooner than ideal, his original prep run having been due over 2 weeks earlier, trouble in running plus prevailing inexperience also counting against him; in touch, labouring before 3 out; worth another chance. **Mister Fisher** was below his best up in grade, not travelling so well in this company as he had previously; waited with, pushed along after fifth, left behind before 2 out. **Vision d'Honneur** in first-time tongue strap, couldn't repeat the improved effort he put up behind the winner at Leopardstown; waited with, ridden before 3 out, never on terms; he's very much the type to make a chaser. **Al Dancer** disappointed, losing his unbeaten record over hurdles, wearing earplugs rather than a hood, his finishing effort a tame one, in contrast to some of his previous races; in touch, took keen hold, went prominent before fifth, ridden 3 out, weakened soon after; he'll surely bounce back from this. **Grand Sancy** disappointed, a failure to get any cover contributing, though it's possible he isn't suited by the track; handy, not settle fully, pushed along before 3 out, weakened soon after; he'll hopefully get a chance to show his true merit at Aintree. **The Big Bite** after 11 weeks off, showed raw potential, just not looking ready for this sort of test when it came to the crunch; handy, not settle fully, mistake fourth, not fluent 3 out, weakened soon after, not knocked about; he needs to grow up but has potential as a novice chaser for next season. **The Flying Sofa** was out of his depth; raced off the pace, tailed off before 3 out. **Beaufort West** was flying too high in this grade; soon behind, pulled up before straight. **Brandon Castle** lost his unbeaten record over hurdles, up considerably in grade, difficult to pull off the tactics that had served him well at a lower level; led until fifth, weakened soon after, pulled up straight. **Normal Norman** was hopelessly out of his depth; raced off the pace, labouring fourth, pulled up.

Racing Post Arkle Challenge Trophy Novices' Chase (Grade 1) (1)

Pos	Btn	Horse	Age	Wgt	Eq	Trainer	Jockey	SP
1		DUC DES GENIEVRES (FR)	6	11-4		W. P. Mullins, Ireland	P. Townend	5/1
2	13	US AND THEM (IRE)	6	11-4	(t)	Joseph Patrick O'Brien, Ireland	J. J. Slevin	14/1
3	3¾	ARTICULUM (IRE)	9	11-4	(t)	Terence O'Brien, Ireland	D. J. Mullins	25/1
4	2¾	CLONDAW CASTLE (IRE)	7	11-4		Tom George	Ciaran Gethings	33/1
5	5	KNOCKNANUSS (IRE)	9	11-4		Gary Moore	Jamie Moore	33/1
6	2¼	PALOMA BLUE (IRE)	7	11-4		Henry de Bromhead, Ireland	Robbie Power	10/1
7	11	HARDLINE (IRE)	7	11-4	(h)	Gordon Elliott, Ireland	Davy Russell	10/3f
8	6	SLATE HOUSE (IRE)	7	11-4	(t)	Colin Tizzard	Harry Cobden	66/1
F		ORNUA (IRE)	8	11-4		Henry de Bromhead, Ireland	Rachael Blackmore	14/1

ur	GLEN FORSA (IRE)	7	11-4	Mick Channon	Jonathan Burke	9/2
ur	KALASHNIKOV (IRE)	6	11-4	Amy Murphy	Jack Quinlan	6/1
pu	LALOR (GER)	7	11-4	Kayley Woollacott	Richard Johnson	13/2

12 ran Race Time 3m 58.70 Closing Sectional (3.75f): 55.4s (101.6%) Winning Owner: Sullivan Bloodstock Limited

The biggest Arkle field since 12 also went to post for Sizing Europe's race in 2010, though the market told the tale of an unusual lack of standouts in the division—a recurring theme in the novice ranks this season—and, in event, it delivered even less for all Duc des Genievres put in a flawless display to rout them, competition to the emphatic winner greatly reduced as the likes of Glen Forsa, Lalor and Kalashnikov were out of it by halfway, the last-named departing in luckless fashion after one had fallen in his path; much of the pre-race talk was of a likely breakneck pace but, with Knocknanuss undone by a standing start after a false one initally and other pace-setting candidates taken back, Ornua didn't have to go hard to establish a lead. **Duc des Genievres** may be set to succeed where many others have hitherto failed and prove capable of giving Altior something of a scare it nothing else, such was the impression left in routing an Arkle field that admittedly began to dissolve from an early stage, erasing any memories of his tame finish in last season's Ballymore as he proved himself a class apart, not just on the day but surely overall in the division as well; reverted to more patient tactics with so many by-trade front runners in opposition, there was barely a moment's doubt with the likes of Glen Forsa and Kalashnikov out of the race by the sixth, moving up into third at the water, still going powerfully when produced to lead 3 out and most impressive as he left for dead those who remained in the straight, already well away when producing another fluent leap at the last for good measure; he'll continue to take all the beating, this side of a clash with the imperious Altior in any case. **Us And Them** looks set to fall short of the best 2-milers but can do well in handicaps or lower-level graded company once his novice status has expired, a model of consistency and durability to date and doing extremely well to force his way to the front of the far more competitive 'race' for second, having found himself a long way back under a change of tactics, a peck at the first compounding matters; he was still only seventh before 3 out, but he finished with such purpose that he'd taken second halfway up the run-in, even appearing to finish with running left at the line. **Articulum** ran about as well as could have been expected upped in grade, benefiting from the shortcomings/misfortune of others to claim an unlikely placing; mid-field, hampered seventh, ridden after 3 out, kept on, took third run-in. **Clondaw Castle** didn't look remotely out of place stepping out of handicaps only for the effort of trying to go with the high-class winner to take its toll, shaping much better than the bare result but enduring a hard race with it, looming up briefly after 3 out and still a clear second—5 lengths ahead of Articulum—at the last before he wilted. **Knocknanuss** had little go right in the race, forced into doing too much too soon after losing ground during the standing start, getting to the front by the sixth but having nothing left once headed 3 out. **Paloma Blue** was found out in better company, not coping anything like as well as in the Supreme last year on his previous Cheltenham visit, perhaps lacking the heart for such demanding fences; mid-field, jumped none too fluently, hampered sixth, lost ground 4 out, shaken up before next, weakened straight. **Hardline** had gone from lively outsider in the lead-up to clear favourite at the off but never looked like justifiying the move, in trouble under a circuit out and never even threatening to make an impression; perhaps a physical issue will come to light, worth noting that he'd given Us And Them a double-digit margin beating himself at Navan before Christmas. **Slate House** had an already very stiff task made hopeless when hampered in the melee at the sixth. **Ornua** forced the early pace as usual but had just been headed when falling at the sixth. **Glen Forsa** found himself already shuffled towards the back when making a most uncharacteristic error at the fourth, unseating his rider; he's well worth another chance at this sort of level, starting with the Manifesto at Aintree, when a smaller field and a return to more positive tactics ought to see him shine as he has before. **Kalashnikov** gave the impression he was right back on his game in time for another Festival bid only to be caught in the slipstream as Ornua fell, giving his rider no chance of staying aboard. **Lalor** had dipped below expectations at Sandown 3 months earlier but this was something else, running so badly he was surely amiss, getting reminders early on the final circuit with no response, losing touch quickly and pulled up some way out.

Unibet Champion Hurdle Challenge Trophy (Grade 1) (1)

Pos	Btn	Horse	Age	Wgt	Eq	Trainer	Jockey	SP
1		ESPOIR D'ALLEN (FR)	5	11-10		Gavin Patrick Cromwell, Ireland	M. P. Walsh	16/1
2	15	MELON	7	11-10	(s)	W. P. Mullins, Ireland	P. Townend	20/1
3	nk	SILVER STREAK (IRE)	6	11-10		Evan Williams	Adam Wedge	80/1
4	1½	LAURINA (FR)	6	11-3		W. P. Mullins, Ireland	R. Walsh	5/2
5	7	VERDANA BLUE (IRE)	7	11-3		Nicky Henderson	Davy Russell	33/1
6	6	APPLE'S JADE (FR)	7	11-3	(t)	Gordon Elliott, Ireland	J. W. Kennedy	7/4f
7	45	GLOBAL CITIZEN (IRE)	7	11-10		Ben Pauling	David Bass	50/1
F		BUVEUR D'AIR (FR)	8	11-10		Nicky Henderson	Barry Geraghty	11/4
bd		SHARJAH (FR)	6	11-10		W. P. Mullins, Ireland	Mr P. W. Mullins	20/1
pu		BRAIN POWER (IRE)	8	11-10	(s)	Nicky Henderson	Nico de Boinville	33/1

10 ran Race Time 3m 59.30 Closing Sectional (4.10f): 61.1s (97.9%) Winning Owner: Mr John P. McManus

Given the widest winning margin in the Champion Hurdle this century, surpassing the 11 lengths by which Rooster Booster won in 2003, Espoir d'Allen's performance is clearly that of a top-class hurdler, yet the race didn't deliver all it promised, none of the trio that dominated the market making the first 3, one falling, one running no race at all and the other just well short of expectations, the lack of depth at the top of the 2m hurdling division continuing to be a cause for concern, particularly with the principals from the Supreme looking more obvious Arkle than Champion Hurdle candidates, the winner at least a 5-y-o, a rare winner for his age group, the first since Katchit in 2008. **Espoir d'Allen** was patently much improved, announcing himself with fanfare up in grade after winning all 3 of his previous starts this season, though to just what extent isn't easy to assess, given so many of his rivals clearly failed to give their running, a slightly more cautious view of the form than might otherwise be the case best taken for now, a repeat at Punchestown hopefully providing a clearer measure of just what he achieved and how dominant a force he can be in the 2m hurdling division; patiently ridden, headway 3 out, led on bridle 2 out, quickened clear, impressive. **Melon** in first-time cheekpieces, finished second at the Festival for the third year running, reviving to a certain extent after a lacklustre campaign, given a more prominent ride, just no match for the winner in the closing stages; led until 2 out, not fluent last, kept on. **Silver Streak** ran about as well as could have been expected upped in grade, connections' enterprise in running well rewarded; dropped out, headway before 3 out, kept on; he's well established as a smart hurdler, though no better. **Laurina** well backed, failed to meet expectations, even if her previous form had an element of style over substance to it; handy, chased leader from fourth, every chance when mistake

3 out, ridden after, no extra before last; she may yet do better, particularly back against her own sex. **Verdana Blue** was well held, doubts about the ground scuppering her chance, her rider keen to handle her as sympathetically as possible; held up, travelled well, still plenty to do before 3 out, some headway before 2 out, no extra straight, not given at all a hard time. **Apple's Jade** strong in the betting and the clear pick on this season's form, disappointed in no uncertain terms, just not travelling anything like so well as usual, being taken on for the lead and the track just incidental to a really poor performance; pressed leader, never travelling well, lost place fourth, no threat soon after. **Global Citizen** was out of his depth; in touch until fifth. **Buveur d'Air** ended his bid for a third Champion Hurdle in anti-climactic fashion; in touch, fell third. **Sharjah** failed to complete, through no fault of his own; held up, brought down third. **Brain Power** ran no sort of race after 13 weeks off, such a performance no real surprise given his overall record, his trainer's excuse about the ground not holding water; held up, never a danger.

CHELTENHAM Wednesday March 13
SOFT

Ballymore Novices' Hurdle (Baring Bingham) (Grade 1) (1)

Pos	Btn	Horse	Age	Wgt	Eq	Trainer	Jockey	SP
1		CITY ISLAND (IRE)	6	11-7	(t)	Martin Brassil, Ireland	M. P. Walsh	8/1
2	2	CHAMP (IRE)	7	11-7		Nicky Henderson	Barry Geraghty	9/2
3	2¼	BRIGHT FORECAST (IRE)	5	11-7		Ben Pauling	Nico de Boinville	25/1
4	1½	BREWIN'UPASTORM (IRE)	6	11-7		Olly Murphy	Richard Johnson	11/1
5	9	SAMS PROFILE	5	11-7		M. F. Morris, Ireland	B. J. Cooper	9/1
6	hd	GALVIN (IRE)	5	11-7		Gordon Elliott, Ireland	Davy Russell	12/1
7	11	SEDDON (IRE)	6	11-7		Tom George	Noel Fehily	33/1
8	1	EASY GAME (FR)	5	11-7		W. P. Mullins, Ireland	R. Walsh	7/1
9	¾	JARVEYS PLATE (IRE)	6	11-7		Fergal O'Brien	Paddy Brennan	20/1
10	1¼	ASK DILLON (IRE)	6	11-7		Fergal O'Brien	Sean Bowen	50/1
11	14	VALDIEU (IRE)	6	11-7	(t)	Noel Meade, Ireland	Sean Flanagan	66/1
12	8	NOTEBOOK (GER)	6	11-7	(t)	Henry de Bromhead, Ireland	Rachael Blackmore	50/1
pu		BATTLEOVERDOYEN (IRE)	6	11-7		Gordon Elliott, Ireland	J. W. Kennedy	3/1f
pu		BEAKSTOWN (IRE)	6	11-7	(t)	Dan Skelton	Harry Skelton	14/1
pu		CASTLEBAWN WEST (IRE)	6	11-7		W. P. Mullins, Ireland	P. Townend	25/1
pu		DUNVEGAN (FR)	6	11-7		P. A. Fahy, Ireland	D. J. Mullins	33/1

16 ran   Race Time 5m 06.60   Closing Sectional (4.10f): 59.8s (100.1%)   Winning Owner: Mrs B. Mulryan

A representative field for one of the feature novice hurdles of the season and it's form that looks well up to scratch, the first 4 finishing clear and grounds for viewing all of them positively, set to make an impact next season whether novice chasing or in open company over hurdles; they were a good-looking bunch, by and large, a stronger field in that regard than the Supreme. **City Island** took the step up in grade in his stride, showing himself among the leaders of his division, clearly more to come as he is further tested, his physique suggesting very much a switch to fences next season, likely to stay 3m but not short of speed; held up, travelled well, headway after sixth, not clear run approaching 3 out, led before last, kept on well. **Champ** was beaten for the first time this season, but confirmed himself a smart young hurdler, really losing nothing in defeat to such a promising rival, more races to be won with him at around this trip, perhaps starting with the Mersey Novices' Hurdle at Aintree; in touch, travelled well, crept closer sixth, led 2 out, ridden soon after, headed before last, kept on well. **Bright Forecast** upped markedly in trip, ran really well upped in grade, the extra distance really playing to his strengths; held up, effort before 2 out, not quicken home turn, kept on well run-in, took third near finish; he's still at an early stage of his career and can be expected to go on again. **Brewin'upastorm** confirmed the form he was showing here last time, even if he came up a little short overall, possibly not so stout a stayer as one or 2 of those ahead of him, definitely the third; held up, travelled well, good progress before 2 out, edged left, not quicken approaching last, lost third near finish; his stable has several other good novice chase prospects for next season, though a switch to fences rather than staying over hurdles seems the most likely route. **Sams Profile** seemed to have his limitations exposed in this company, having his chance but not good enough to go with the principals into the straight; handy, every chance when not fluent 2 out, weakened straight; he's one of the less imposing sorts in this field, though has won a point, so may well find his way over fences next season. **Galvin** upped markedly in trip, shaped better than the bare result, his jumping letting him down at crucial stages, likely to be well suited by this trip another day; held up, mistake sixth, headway when mistake 3 out, not quicken straight. **Seddon** was below form up in grade, though he shaped better than the bare result, not unusual for him; led until not fluent seventh, weakened after 2 out, eased last; there's a smart horse in there, trying to get out, perhaps that will happen over fences next season. **Easy Game** well backed, seemed to find the company beyond him, spared a hard race once his chance had gone; held up, travelled well, shaken up before 2 out, made no impression, not knocked about; likely the majority of these, he looks the sort to make an impact as a novice chaser next season. **Jarveys Plate** had had his limitations exposed last time and never really looked likely to land a blow; mid-division, labouring before 3 out. **Ask Dillon** was flying too high at this stage of his hurdling career, never competitive after taking a long time to warm to his task; in rear, mistake first, effort when mistake 3 out, left behind soon after. **Valdieu** upped markedly in trip and on softer ground than previously, fared no better than on his previous try in Grade 1 company; close up, travelled well, led seventh, headed 2 out, left behind soon after. **Notebook** was well held up in grade; mid-division, ridden before 3 out, left behind before next; he has the physique to make a chaser. **Battleoverdoyen** well backed, is just the most gorgeous-looking horse but failed to run any sort of race, reported to have lost a shoe; mid-field, off the bridle long way out, left behind 3 out; hopefully, he will bounce back quickly, as he had looked an exciting prospect prior to this. **Beakstown** ran poorly, stopping as if all might not have been well; prominent, weakened quickly 3 out, pulled up straight; he has the physique to make a chaser. **Castlebawn West** failed to complete, though the run is best ignored, other than that his jumping needs work; raced off the pace, travelled well, bad mistake fifth, still plenty to do before 3 out, blundered there, pulled up straight, not given at all a hard time; he remains with potential. **Dunvegan** fared no better than last time, clearly with something to prove after his 2 starts at this level; handy, weakened before 3 out, pulled up straight.

RSA Insurance Novices' Chase (Grade 1) (1)

Pos	Btn	Horse	Age	Wgt	Eq	Trainer	Jockey	SP
1		TOPOFTHEGAME (IRE)	7	11-4	(t)	Paul Nicholls	Harry Cobden	4/1
2	½	SANTINI	7	11-4		Nicky Henderson	Nico de Boinville	3/1
3	1¾	DELTA WORK (FR)	6	11-4	(h+t)	Gordon Elliott, Ireland	Davy Russell	15/8f
4	16	MISTER MALARKY	6	11-4		Colin Tizzard	Robbie Power	20/1
5	½	MORTAL (IRE)	7	11-4	(t)	Joseph Patrick O'Brien, Ireland	Rachael Blackmore	20/1
6	2	DROVERS LANE (IRE)	7	11-4		Rebecca Curtis	Sean Bowen	20/1

7	6	COUNT MERIBEL	7	11-4		Nigel Twiston-Davies	Mark Grant		66/1
8	1	NOW MCGINTY (IRE)	8	11-4	(s)	Stuart Edmunds	Tom O'Brien		33/1
F		TOP VILLE BEN (IRE)	7	11-4	(h)	Philip Kirby	Sean Quinlan		33/1
pu		DRINKS INTERVAL	7	10-11	(t)	Colin Tizzard	Richard Johnson		100/1
pu		ON THE BLIND SIDE (IRE)	7	11-4	(s)	Nicky Henderson	Noel Fehily		14/1
pu		THE WORLDS END (IRE)	8	11-4	(s)	Tom George	Paddy Brennan		16/1

12 ran Race Time 6m 18.30 Closing Sectional (3.75f): 55.4s (105.1%) Winning Owner: Mr Chris Giles & Mr&Mrs P K Barber

The most satisfying race of the first 2 days of the Festival, with all the leading contenders showing their form, the trio that dominated the market pulling well clear of their rivals after plenty looked in with a chance 3 out, no reason to think that they are anything other than well up to standard for the race and major contenders for top honours in staying chases next season, though it should be pointed out that La Bague Au Roi had beaten the first 2 in the Kauto Star and might well have been hard to beat here, though connections of the beaten horses might also have hopes of turning the tables on the winner another day. **Topofthegame** had been just denied in the Coral Cup on this card in 2018 and went one better under a superb ride, produced later than at Kempton; patiently ridden, travelled well, not fluent tenth, tracked pace entering straight, led soon after last, kept on, ridden out; he's been sparingly raced so far, so presumably wouldn't be a likely candidate for Aintree or Punchestown, perhaps something like the Ladbroke Trophy the next time he'll be seen—he should do well in 2019/20 and it would be no surprise were he to develop into a top Gold Cup contender. **Santini** had finished behind the winner in the Kauto Star and did so again, despite the track seemingly much more in his favour than Kempton had been, perhaps his much-publicized problems with his shoes over the weekend a factor, though he had every chance on the face of it, not much between the first 2, if not 3; handy, travelled well, stumbled soon after 4 out, every chance from 3 out, shaken up straight, led 2 out, headed soon after last, kept on; he'll continue to progress, this just his third start over fences, and a rematch with La Bague Au Roi in the Mildmay would be a race to savour. **Delta Work** lost his unbeaten record over fences in the toughest race he's contested, though he emerged with plenty of credit, cutting out jumping errors likely to be key in his chance of turning the tables on the first 2; in touch, travelled well, mistake second, mistake 4 out, led next, headed 2 out, not quicken last; he will presumably bid to gain consolation in the Grade 1 at Punchestown in May, definitely with more to offer. **Mister Malarky** would definitely have made more impact in the NH Chase, rather outclassed at the business end yet still emerging with credit, a likely sort to win a good handicap over long distances at some stage; held up, not fluent second, pushed along fifteenth, headway before 3 out, left behind straight. **Mortal** ran up to his best, just briefly threatening to play a bigger role than he ultimately did; held up, pushed along fifteenth, headway after 3 out, every chance briefly 2 out, weakened; he's shown himself a useful novice this winter, still only 4 runs into his chasing career, and he's likely to have a future in handicaps. **Drovers Lane** who'd had a breathing operation, ran about as well as could have been expected upped in grade; waited with, headway 4 out, every chance after 3 out, mistake 2 out, weakened; he has a future as a useful handicapper. **Count Meribel** back up in trip after 12 weeks off, needed to improve to make an impact in this grade and wasn't up to the task, his future lying in handicaps; in touch, mistake seventh, labouring 4 out. **Now McGinty** would have been better off in the NH Chase, though he didn't run as if on his game anyway; chased leaders, labouring fourteenth. **Top Ville Ben** back left handed, didn't get very far;

prominent, fell heavily sixth. **Drinks Interval** was found out in better company, though a change of plan at the fourth probably did her no favours; held up, jumped well in main, rapid headway to lead fourth, headed after 3 out, weakened quickly, pulled up straight. **On The Blind Side** in first-time cheekpieces, seemed to resent them and ran no sort of race; soon behind, never travelling well, pulled up before thirteenth. **The Worlds End** again failed to confirm earlier promise, though had an excuse, reported lame; led until fourth, remained prominent, weakened 3 out, pulled up straight.

Betway Queen Mother Champion Chase (Grade 1) (1)

Pos	Btn	Horse	Age	Wgt	Eq	Trainer	Jockey	SP
1		ALTIOR (IRE)	9	11-10		Nicky Henderson	Nico de Boinville	4/11f
2	1¾	POLITOLOGUE (FR)	8	11-10	(h+t)	Paul Nicholls	Harry Cobden	11/1
3	1¾	SCEAU ROYAL (FR)	7	11-10		Alan King	Daryl Jacob	16/1
4	6	HELL'S KITCHEN	8	11-10	(h+t)	Harry Fry	Barry Geraghty	25/1
5	1¾	MIN (FR)	8	11-10		W. P. Mullins, Ireland	R. Walsh	7/2
6	8	CASTLEGRACE PADDY (IRE)	8	11-10		P. A. Fahy, Ireland	Davy Russell	25/1
7	5	SAINT CALVADOS (FR)	6	11-10	(s)	Harry Whittington	Gavin Sheehan	25/1
8	10	ORDINARY WORLD (IRE)	9	11-10		Henry de Bromhead, Ireland	Rachael Blackmore	33/1
pu		GOD'S OWN (IRE)	11	11-10		Tom George	Paddy Brennan	16/1

9 ran Race Time 3m 59.40 Closing Sectional (3.75f): 55.5s (101.7%) Winning Owner: Mrs Patricia Pugh

The lack of depth in the 2m division—Saint Calvados was the only one in the line-up who'd contested the previous year's Arkle—meant this was largely a re-run of the 2018 renewal, none of the vanquished quartet who were back for more with obvious chances of turning the tables on Altior, and it was left to a second-season chaser who'd been forced to miss last year's Arkle to provide the biggest threat to the holder's crown, Sceau Royal even hitting the front at the last; an interesting tactical battle played out after Saint Calvados and Altior had stolen a march on their rivals at the start, the rest happy to wait in behind, even once Altior had hit the front after the third last, Jacob leaving it as late as he dared on Sceau Royal but even that proved too early; the proximity of the placed horses, as well as Hell's Kitchen in fourth, means it's hard to escape the conclusion that Altior was some way below his best on the day, though he was still recording his fourth Festival success—a feat remarkably matched by Tiger Roll just 40 minutes later. **Altior** wasn't at his best after 8 weeks off, the tacky ground perhaps part of the reason, and he was given a real fright as a result, but overcame it to become the fourth dual Champion Chase winner this century, matching the sequence of 18 successive wins that Big Buck's managed in the process; he tracked Saint Calvados, several lengths clear of the rest, jumping superbly until a mistake at the water, also guessing a touch at the third last prior to hitting the front and not seeing a stride at either of the last 2 fences, pounced upon at the last before quickly rallying to regain the lead and typically finding plenty up the hill to assert in the final 100 yds; even in running below par he showed just why he's so hard to beat and, though the clamour to step him up in trip will remain, a hard race here might put a crack at the Melling Chase in doubt, while the 3m division is far more packed at the top than the 2m one—several very good novices throwing their hats into that particular ring earlier this afternoon too—and it's easy to see him sticking to this sort of trip for a while yet, a possible clash with Cyrname in the Celebration at Sandown likely to be something to savour. **Politologue** had never been at his best at Cheltenham in the past (beaten 23 lengths in this race the year before) but, back at 2m for the first time this season and with the hood back on, ran right up to the pick of his form having attracted some support, providing a significant boost to Cyrname in the process; he lined up to track the leaders but didn't get away too well, meaning he was settled in mid-division, was close up by the third last and still going well when brushing through the next, brought to challenge at the last and briefly holding every chance but not quite able to match Altior up the hill, still seeing the race out well himself for second; this puts him on the front foot for a repeat bid in the Melling. **Sceau Royal** clearly all the better for his tune-up over hurdles, ran a cracker back at Cheltenham, surpassing the level of form that saw him win the Shloer in the autumn, even trading as low as 1.6 in-running as he jumped on at the last and, still a young horse in the context of this race, may yet prove a bigger threat to Altior another day, notwithstanding the winner was plainly below his best; he jumped low and quickly in touch up the inner, made headway on the bridle approaching the home turn and, having been close up over the second last, was produced to lead at the last, understandably not quite as strong as the first pair up the hill but clear of the rest; he could be one for Punchestown. **Hell's Kitchen** was up significantly in grade having won a handicap from a BHA mark of 143 when last seen 12 weeks earlier and acquitted himself well, even if not quite able to reproduce his Ascot rating, ridden very differently this time; held up, progress approaching the home turn, went fourth soon after the second last and kept on in the wake of the principals to readily fend off a below-par Min for that position. **Min** seemingly the only legitimate challenger to Altior again having won Grade 1 events on his 2 previous outings this campaign, failed to give his running this time around, no issue immediately coming to light; he was a bit keen under restraint in mid-field with Walsh seemingly keen to delay his challenge, still waiting on the run to the third last, but it was obvious that Min wasn't going that well when he was shuffled back before the home turn and he was held by the second last; the fact that he's been beaten 7 lengths or more on each visit to Cheltenham is mis-representative of his talent. **Castlegrace Paddy** an early faller when last seen, shaped better than the distance beaten suggests, just not getting up the hill for whatever reason; held up, he took a keen hold and nodded at the sixth but crept closer after 3 out and was on the heels of the leaders at the next before wilting. **Saint Calvados** was well held in first-time cheekpieces, possibly overdoing things in front though he's been put in his place at Grade 1 level since seeing off Footpad on his return; led, steadied into second, headed soon after 3 out, weakened. **Ordinary World** fared no better than in the race last year, losing touch in the back straight and never a threat. **God's Own** after 3 months off, shaped better than being pulled up might suggest running in the race for a fourth time, previously finishing fourth, fifth and third respectively and looking set for one of those minor placings again until pulling up sharply before the last, reportedly lame.

Weatherbys Champion Bumper (Standard Open National Hunt Flat) (Grade 1) (1)

Pos	Btn	Horse	Age	Wgt	Eq	Trainer	Jockey	SP
1		ENVOI ALLEN (FR)	5	11-5		Gordon Elliott, Ireland	Mr J. J. Codd	2/1f
2	¾	BLUE SARI (FR)	4	10-11		W. P. Mullins, Ireland	Barry Geraghty	7/2
3	1¾	THYME HILL	5	11-5		Philip Hobbs	Richard Johnson	20/1
4	3¼	ABACADABRAS (FR)	5	11-5		Gordon Elliott, Ireland	Ms L. O'Neill	14/1
5	1½	THE GLANCING QUEEN (IRE)	5	10-12		Alan King	Wayne Hutchinson	20/1
6	½	SEMPO (IRE)	5	11-5	(t)	Joseph Patrick O'Brien, Ireland	Mr Derek O'Connor	12/1
7	9	SOME DETAIL (IRE)	5	11-5		Nigel Hawke	Sean Bowen	100/1
8	sh	METICULOUS (IRE)	5	11-5	(t)	Joseph Patrick O'Brien, Ireland	Donnacha O'Brien	7/1
9	¾	ASK FOR GLORY (IRE)	5	11-5		Paul Nicholls	Harry Cobden	13/2
10	2	FLIC OU VOYOU (FR)	5	11-5		Paul Nicholls	Sam Twiston-Davies	33/1

11	1¼	THOR DE CERISY (FR)	5	11-5	(h)	Michael Scudamore	Brendan Powell	100/1
12	nk	MASTER DEBONAIR	5	11-5		Colin Tizzard	Robbie Power	12/1
13	¾	CASCOVA (IRE)	4	10-11		Martyn Meade	Noel Fehily	66/1
14	1	JELSKI (GER)	5	11-5		Nigel Twiston-Davies	Jamie Bargary	66/1

14 ran Race Time 3m 55.60 Closing Sectional (3.90f): 56.3s (99.5%) Winning Owner: Cheveley Park Stud

A much smaller field than before for the Champion Bumper and not the depth of form that might be expected coming into the race, the British challenge looking decidedly thin, Irish stables dominating as so often, even though Willie Mullins had just one runner rather than, as more usually, a handful, the first 2—presumably—expensive purchases and smart prospects—probably better in relation to the rest than the bare result, the runner-up perhaps even denied victory when losing his action very late on; the field was still well grouped approaching the straight, the tempo picking up fully only at that point. **Envoi Allen** well backed, made it 4 wins from 4 starts in bumpers, handling the softer ground well, clearly a leading novice hurdle prospect for next season, plenty to like about the way he knuckled down when tackled; waited with, travelled well, headway 4f out, led over 3f out, quickened straight, joined 1f out, kept on, in command final 100 yds. **Blue Sari** who had changed hands since his impressive debut, looked a good prospect in pressing the winner so close, perhaps unlucky in that he went lame very late on; held up, effort over 3f out, chased leader entering straight, challenged final 1f, no extra final 50 yds; hopefully the problem won't be one to keep him off the track and he'll make into a smart novice hurdler next season. **Thyme Hill** emerged comfortably best of the British-trained runners, his form better than the market suggested and reasons for thinking him better than the result last time, though this still represents signficant further improvement; prominent, ridden approaching straight, not quicken, kept on inside final 1f; he's likely to be more about stamina than speed over hurdles, but he should do well as a novice next season. **Abacadabras** probably has as much ability as the first 2, but his attitude is lacking at this stage and he threw his chance away again; in touch, travelled well, smooth headway over 4f out, every chance entering straight, ridden, wandered badly, no extra final 1f. **The Glancing Queen** matched previous form, shaping better than the bare result as well, stuck in traffic on the approach to the straight and never able to land a blow; held up, travelled well, effort approaching straight, short of room, stayed on straight, nearest at the finish; she'd be a leading contender for the Nickel Coin next month, if over these exertions. **Sempo** continued his run-to-run progression, producing a smart effort up in grade; held up, travelled well, headway approaching straight, ridden 2f out, not quicken; he should fill out over the summer and has built a good foundation for novice hurdling. **Some Detail** ran about as well as could have been expected upped in grade, though he very much had the run of the race and may prove slightly flattered; led, ridden when headed over 3f out, weakened. **Meticulous** on softer ground than previously, had a top Flat jockey taking over in the saddle, but he wasn't in the same form as last time, not far behind the winner on that occasion; prominent, took keen hold, ridden approaching straight, outpaced soon after; he has plenty to recommend him as a prospective jumper, including probably the best pedigree in the field. **Ask For Glory** was the shortest-priced of the British-trained runners, but he failed to repeat his highly promising debut form, a change of tactics possibly not helping; in touch, not settle fully, lost place over 3f out; he's got potential as a novice hurdler for next season. **Flic Ou Voyou** failed to match his improved effort from last time in this more exacting company, ridden more patiently; in touch, ridden approaching straight, weakened soon after; he's got plenty to recommend him as a novice hurdler for next season, not least his physique. **Thor de Cerisy** hasn't gone on from his taking debut and, in a first-time hood, didn't look straightforward to boot, something to prove when he goes jumping; held up, took keen hold, ridden over 4f out, looked none too keen. **Master Debonair** had the same chance as the third on their running here in November, but he wasn't in the same form, doing too much for his own good; close up, not settle fully, weakened over 3f out. **Cascova** gelded since last seen, faced a stiff task in this grade over a longer trip and never looked likely to get involved; in rear, ridden 4f out, edged right, made no impression; he's as good looking as any of this field, though his future may well be on the Flat rather than over jumps, given his yard. **Jelski** found the company well beyond him; held up, labouring end of back straight; he's not a bad type and has potential as a novice hurdler at a more realistic level next season.

CHELTENHAM Thursday March 14
GOOD to SOFT

JLT Novices' Chase (Golden Miller) (Grade 1) (1)

Pos	Btn	Horse	Age	Wgt	Eq	Trainer	Jockey	SP
1		DEFI DU SEUIL (FR)	6	11-4		Philip Hobbs	Barry Geraghty	3/1f
2	2¼	LOSTINTRANSLATION (IRE)	7	11-4		Colin Tizzard	Robbie Power	4/1
3	7	MENGLI KHAN (IRE)	6	11-4	(t)	Gordon Elliott, Ireland	J. W. Kennedy	9/1
4	3	KILDISART (IRE)	7	11-4		Ben Pauling	Daryl Jacob	9/1
5	ns	VINNDICATION (IRE)	6	11-4		Kim Bailey	David Bass	11/2
6	6	REAL STEEL (FR)	6	11-4		W. P. Mullins, Ireland	P. Townend	13/2
7	6	CASTAFIORE (USA)	6	10-11	(s)	Charlie Longsdon	Paul O'Brien	33/1
8	15	CAPELAND (FR)	7	11-4	(t)	Paul Nicholls	Harry Cobden	28/1
9	40	PRAVALAGUNA (FR)	7	10-11		W. P. Mullins, Ireland	D. J. Mullins	14/1
ur		VOIX DU REVE (FR)	7	11-4	(h)	W. P. Mullins, Ireland	R. Walsh	9/1

10 ran Race Time 5m 01.00 Closing Sectional (4.00f): 55.1s (110.6%) Winning Owner: Mr John P. McManus

The personal score between Defi du Seuil and Lostintranslation this season stood at one apiece and there was little to separate them in the market once again, the pair confirming themselves very smart novices as they cleared away from the rest from the second last, Defi du Seuil's superior gears the difference between them once again on this occasion after Lostintranslation had set just a fair gallop, while a few of those in behind found jumping blemishes preventing them making more of an impact; overall the form was slightly below that of the winners of the Arkle and the RSA earlier in the week. **Defi du Seuil** confirmed Sandown form with the runner-up and is clearly a very smart novice, things going very smoothly for him and no danger of letting Lostintranslation back in once he'd hit the front this time; settled in mid-field, he screwed at the second but was generally very good, jumped into a handy position at the eleventh, loomed up at the second last and, though not quite as quick over it as the first pair, was produced to challenge at the last, showing a better turn of foot than the runner-up from there to win readily; after an inauspicious start over fences he's done nothing but improve and looks well capable of bridging the gap to open Grade 1 class at this sort of trip next season. **Lostintranslation** might have lost the decider in his personal battle with Defi du Seuil but emerges with both his rating and reputation enhanced, the winner just better equipped for this sort of test, Lostintranslation very much the type to up his game further over 3m+ next season; he jumped soundly out in front, setting no more than a fair gallop, pressed on from the second last before being tackled at the final fence, unable to match the winner's turn of foot on the run-in but continuing to draw clear of the rest. **Mengli Khan** got back on the up to fill the same spot as in the Supreme last year, at least matching that level of form, just not as strong a stayer at this trip as the first pair; having raced handily and travelled fluently, he was close up when pecking at the third last but still held every chance at the next before unable to live with the first pair from there; he'll have a better chance at this level back home for the remainder of the spring. **Kildisart** ran to a similar level as when winning the novice handicap on Trials' Day 7 weeks earlier, having much more on in this company, particularly with his jumping continuing to cost him a little momentum here and there; racing on the outer in mid-division, he wasn't fluent at the tenth and again 4 out, made his effort from the next but couldn't quicken early in straight, not fluent once more 2 out and lacking the pace to make much of an impression, though did edge out Vinndication for fourth. **Vinndication** who was allowed to take his chance after pleasing connections at home the week before (having initially been ruled out of the Festival), ostensibly wasn't up to the task, beaten further by the first pair than at Sandown, his jumping not standing the test going left-handed for the first time; chasing the leader, he wasn't fluent at the second before belting the fourth, also slow at the eleventh, switching outside the leaders approaching the third last, pecking there and unable to go with the principals soon after, plugging on very much in the style of a stayer; the sooner he gets over 3m+ the better. **Real Steel** is best not judged too harshly on this run up in grade, always likely to struggle given the magnitude of his stumble at halfway; patiently ridden, he wasn't fluent at the fourth and stumbled badly at the seventh, and, though he'd got into contention at the third last, had nothing left from the next; he's well worth another chance in this company. **Castafiore** is better judged on previous form, her Haydock win having been well advertised since, struggling to hold her position in this better company, on a very different track to those on which she'd been running, too; set off handily but soon had to settle in touch, not fluent sixth, struggling after 4 out, faded from home turn. **Capeland** steadily progressive in handicaps this season, was supplemented for this but didn't get a chance to show what he could do, still off the pace when making a mess of 4 out, no threat thereafter. **Pravalaguna** ran poorly upped markedly in grade and ridden very differently, said to have returned with a wound to a heel; held up, untidy 4 out, left behind from next. **Voix du Reve** upped in trip, made a mistake at the first (Walsh nearly unseated) but crept closer at the tenth and was yet to be asked for his effort when unseating at the third last.

Ryanair Chase (Festival Trophy) (Grade 1) (1)

Pos	Btn	Horse	Age	Wgt	Eq	Trainer	Jockey	SP
1		FRODON (FR)	7	11-10	(t)	Paul Nicholls	Bryony Frost	9/2
2	1¼	ASO (FR)	9	11-10		Venetia Williams	Charlie Deutsch	33/1
3	1¾	ROAD TO RESPECT (IRE)	8	11-10		Noel Meade, Ireland	Sean Flanagan	9/2
4	2¼	MONALEE (IRE)	8	11-10		Henry de Bromhead, Ireland	Rachael Blackmore	5/1
5	3¼	UN DE SCEAUX (FR)	11	11-10		W. P. Mullins, Ireland	P. Townend	5/1
6	5	CONEY ISLAND (IRE)	8	11-10	(t)	Edward P. Harty, Ireland	M. P. Walsh	25/1
7	9	BALKO DES FLOS (FR)	8	11-10		Henry de Bromhead, Ireland	Denis O'Regan	16/1
8	3½	FOOTPAD (FR)	7	11-10		W. P. Mullins, Ireland	R. Walsh	7/2f
pu		CHARBEL (IRE)	8	11-10	(s+t)	Kim Bailey	David Bass	40/1
pu		SUB LIEUTENANT (IRE)	10	11-10	(s+t)	Henry de Bromhead, Ireland	J. J. Slevin	66/1

pu	TERREFORT (FR)	6	11-10	Nicky Henderson	Daryl Jacob	20/1
pu	THE STORYTELLER (IRE)	8	11-10	Gordon Elliott, Ireland	Davy Russell	20/1

12 ran Race Time 5m 10.30 Closing Sectional (4.00f): 59.3s (101.7%) Winning Owner: Mr P. J. Vogt

This looked one of the strongest fields assembled for the Ryanair, the first time that 5 horses with a Timeform rating of 165 or above had contested the race, yet it didn't quite live up to expectations, as so often on this track the advantage seeming to lie with those who raced handily, the pair of previous winners both clearly below their best with Footpad failing to return to his form of the year before too, though that's not to take too much away from the hugely tough and likeable winner who had to dig very deep, Bryony Frost becoming the first female rider to win a Grade 1 at Cheltenham. **Frodon** has a superb record on the New Course here and, though strictly speaking not needing to advance his form to record a first Grade 1, deserves plenty of praise for the way he's consistently run to a top-class level this season, produced at his peak 7 weeks on from a gutsy success in the Cotswold Chase, and he's an ongoing credit to not just his rider—who became the first female to win a Grade 1 at Cheltenham—but also his trainer, who made the right call to revert to this race when a crack at the Gold Cup had seemed on the cards, Frodon having first appeared at the Festival in the 2016 Triumph Hurdle alongside stablemate Clan des Obeaux; leading but closely pressed throughout, he typically jumped superbly, was headed at the second last but rallied to lead again soon after the last and proved ultra-game up the hill; it would make sense to draw stumps for the season given how much he's achieved and, still only 7, there's a chance that we haven't yet seen the best of him, a crack at the Gold Cup next year potentially in the offing. **Aso** has been better than ever this season and took his form up a notch further to be placed in this race for the second time, bouncing straight back from an underwhelming run in the Ascot Chase, the second also-ran that day to go on and finish second in a championship race this week; he jumped well and, having tracked the pace, went prominent 5 out, jumping on at the second last before repassed by Frodon after the last, staying on gallantly behind the teak-tough winner; he would seem an obvious candidate for Aintree but hasn't performed well there in the past. **Road To Respect** fourth in the Gold Cup last year and with little obvious chance of improving on that this time around, was re-routed to this shorter option (ran away with the Plate over this C&D in 2017) and, having raced in touch, was close up when clouting the third last, still holding every chance when not fluent at the next, lugging left from there and unable to quicken on the run-in; it's hard to say quite how much the blunder 3 out cost him but the evidence is mounting that he falls just shy of the very best 2½m-3m chasers around. **Monalee** failed to build on his Gowran win, travelling comfortably behind the pace for a long way but one paced after hitting the second last; he falls rather between 2 stools trip-wise, though perhaps a return to 3m at Aintree would see him to better effect. **Un de Sceaux** first and second in this race for the previous 2 years, wasn't at his best this time around, lack of fitness perhaps to blame given the prevailing ground had limited him to just one previous outing this season (3 months earlier); he took a keen hold in mid-field, wasn't fluent at the twelfth and was briefly denied a clear run approaching 4 out, but was in contention at the next before unable to quicken between the last 2; despite his age it wouldn't be a surprise were he to bounce back next time. **Coney Island** in first-time tongue strap after 11 weeks off, wasn't seen to best effect back down in trip, the race—like many on this course—not suiting those held up; patiently ridden, shaken up 5 out, some headway 3 out, kept on but never a threat to principals; he hasn't hit the heights that his novice season suggested he would but he's not one to dismiss out of hand. **Balko des Flos** hasn't gone on from his win in this last year, his third in the John Durkan very much a standout among his efforts since, and he fared no better than when down the field in the Savills Chase 11 weeks earlier; mid-division, untidy fourth, awkward tenth, left behind from 3 out. **Footpad** hasn't hit anything like the heights that his all-conquering novice campaign suggested he would, his season one of issues thus far (suffering over-reaches at both Naas and Leopardstown) and another seemed to surface after 11 weeks off as he was reported to have bled; waited with over this longer trip, he travelled smoothly and had moved into contention after the third last but found little from the next; patience is wearing a little thin but he's in the best hands to come back firing next season. **Charbel** back in a tongue tie, made a string of mistakes and lost touch from the twelfth, eventually pulled up before the third last. **Sub Lieutenant** followed a good run with a below-par one after 7 weeks off, bustled up to press Frodon in front (reminders after a rather slow jump at the first), losing ground 4 out and soon weakening right out of things. **Terrefort** wasn't far behind the winner in the Cotswold Chase but was put well in his place by Clan des Obeaux at Ascot and just ran poorly this time back down in trip/reverted to patient tactics, already struggling before 4 out and left behind from there. **The Storyteller** winner of the Plate on this card last year, has had his limitations exposed at the top level this season and made little impact back down in trip, his jumping a factor in that; racing well off the pace, he made mistakes at the fourth and eleventh, was creeping closer when blundering 5 out and was already held when jumping right 3 out.

Sun Racing Stayers' Hurdle (Grade 1) (1)

Pos	Btn	Horse	Age	Wgt	Eq	Trainer	Jockey	SP
1		PAISLEY PARK (IRE)	7	11-10		Emma Lavelle	Aidan Coleman	11/8f
2	2¾	SAM SPINNER	7	11-10	(s)	Jedd O'Keeffe	Joe Colliver	33/1
3	4	FAUGHEEN (IRE)	11	11-10		W. P. Mullins, Ireland	R. Walsh	4/1
4	1¼	BAPAUME (FR)	6	11-10		W. P. Mullins, Ireland	P. Townend	16/1
5	11	WHOLESTONE (IRE)	8	11-10		Nigel Twiston-Davies	Sam Twiston-Davies	33/1
6	3½	BACARDYS (FR)	8	11-10		W. P. Mullins, Ireland	Mr P. W. Mullins	20/1
7	1¼	SUPASUNDAE	9	11-10	(t)	Mrs J. Harrington, Ireland	Robbie Power	9/1
8	1¼	THE MIGHTY DON (IRE)	7	11-10		Nick Gifford	Leighton Aspell	66/1
9	6	WEST APPROACH	9	11-10		Colin Tizzard	Tom Scudamore	33/1
10	2½	KEEPER HILL (IRE)	8	11-10		Warren Greatrex	Richard Johnson	66/1
11	2	KILBRICKEN STORM (IRE)	8	11-10	(t)	Colin Tizzard	Harry Cobden	16/1
12	2¼	BLACK OP (IRE)	8	11-10	(t)	Tom George	Noel Fehily	14/1
13	½	YANWORTH	9	11-10	(b)	Alan King	Barry Geraghty	33/1
14	¾	PETIT MOUCHOIR (FR)	8	11-10		Henry de Bromhead, Ireland	Rachael Blackmore	25/1
15	¾	TOP NOTCH (FR)	8	11-10		Nicky Henderson	Daryl Jacob	12/1
16	4	MAN OF PLENTY	10	11-10	(b+t)	Sophie Leech	Jonathan Burke	200/1
17	13	COQUIN MANS (FR)	7	11-10		W. P. Mullins, Ireland	D. J. Mullins	100/1
18	15	NAUTICAL NITWIT (IRE)	8	11-10	(s)	Philip Kirby	Thomas Dowson	100/1

18 ran Race Time 5m 52.80 Closing Sectional (3.7f): 55.6s (97.9%) Winning Owner: Mr Andrew Gemmell

This season's Stayers' saw the biggest field assembled in the race since its second running in its alter-ego as the World Hurdle in 2006, the increase in representation perhaps an apparent reflection—and an entirely wrong one as it turned out—of a perceived lack of a star in the division, with any number of a largely rag-tag bunch either recent converts from chasing, overmatched handicappers or uncertain stayers; the pace steadied briefly over a circuit out but that was just about the only let-up in a punishing race that tested all the attributes that should be at a premium in the leading staying hurdle prize in the calendar, the examination drawing top-class efforts—despite the negatives to the depth of the race as a whole—from a comparatively youthful, strong-staying front pair comprised of a runner-up who'd threatened to carry all before him in the division last season and the one who very much has this time around. **Paisley Park** has gone from a coming force to a potentially imperious figure in the division for years to come, capping an unblemished season of irresistible progress in perfect—and now-trademark—fashion, yet to quite reach the exalted levels of, say, Baracouda or Big Buck's but bearing more than a passing resemblance to the latter in particular, the sequence of his extraordinary surge to the front—having turned in around 7 lengths down with as many rivals ahead of him—and subsequent recovery from a blunder at the last so stunning it ought to become a mainstay of any Festival highlights reel, no less stirring visually than such as the 1989 Gold Cup or the 2000 Champion Chase, freakish brilliance from a mere 7-y-o who'll surely add his name to the list of multiple winners of a race with an abundance of memorable renewals this century alone—even this needn't prove his limit. **Sam Spinner** ran into a rival doing what many expected of Sam Spinner in this 12 months earlier but fully restored his status as a top-class stayer in defeat all the same, given the sort of ride that brings out the best in him and, almost as crucially, keeping mistakes to a minimum; content to chase Nautical Nitwit early, he put his foot down to edge ahead 5 out, rallied splendidly to see off Faugheen's challenge from the second last and didn't give in even after Paisley Park had overwhelmed him running to the last, briefly given a second chance by the winner's error there but unable to take advantage, losing nothing in defeat. **Faugheen** added a Stayers' Hurdle placing to a Festival record already featuring wins at 21f (Baring Bingham) and 2m (Champion Hurdle), not the brilliant force of old but still a high-class hurdler whose career has received a new lease of life since attentions have been turned to longer distances, briefly looking to be going best here as he loomed up 2 out but not failing for stamina, reclaiming third from his connections' other representative inside the final 100 yards, a pair of 4-year younger rivals gone by then. **Bapaume** would probably have emerged first in the battle of the Mullins/Ricci pair had his run from rear started sooner but, either way, came out of his toughest test yet with his reputation enhanced, not looking at all out of place at the level and with time on his side to remain a firm fixture on the staying scene; dropped out, he still had the majority ahead of him before 2 out but had made enough headway in the straight to see him dispute third from the last, cracking only late on as the big move told. **Wholestone** put a rare Cheltenham dud behind him 7 weeks on whilst underlining his vulnerability in such lofty company; mid-field, went prominent approaching 2 out, pushed along end of back straight, left behind straight. **Bacardys** still has plenty to offer despite his chequered record, not ridden to best advantage switched from chasing for this after a break (11 weeks) for the second year in a row, back with the rags while still going well 2 out and doing all he could in the straight, passing a good few and finishing with running left; perhaps he can have something to show from a visit to Punchestown, having won there as a novice and arrived on the back of a fall in this when bombing out last year. **Supasundae** edged out by Penhill in a sprint finish to this 12 months earlier, seemed to fail badly for stamina in a far more exacting renewal, though he was fitted with a tongue tie for the first time, either way capitulating so spectacularly he couldn't be entertained if turning up at Aintree or Punchestown (never mind both, as campaigned in 2017/18); mid-field, shaken up before 2 out, effort home turn, third early in straight, stopped quickly, had a hard race. **The Mighty Don** without the headgear worn in the Cleeve, ran better than then but only as well as entitled to, his development having hit a wall since his sights were raised; raced off the pace, mistake fourth, shaken up before 2 out, carried head bit awkwardly straight, made little impression. **West Approach** couldn't maintain his run of getting closest to Paisley Park, the signs of a below-par display clear a fair way out; mid-field, lost ground back straight, rallied briefly end of back straight, effort flattened out. **Keeper Hill** was out of his depth; mid-division, lost ground before 5 out, no chance 2 out, merely plugged on. **Kilbricken Storm** yet another good-quality Tizzard-trained novice chaser switched back to hurdling in recent times, gave cause for encouragement for a long way in his bid for back-to-back Festival successes before disappointing off the bridle, closing in 2 out only to hang left and falter once ridden approaching the straight, perhaps still ailed by something following his problem at Newbury when last seen pre-Christmas. **Black Op** shaped similarly to in the Cleeve, unsuited by the emphasis on stamina; mid-division, mid-race mistakes, driven approaching straight, weakened; will benefit from return to shorter than 3m. **Yanworth** at least shaped a bit better than first time back tried in blinkers; held up, early mistakes, no chance 2 out but at no stage unduly punished; next run should reveal even more. **Petit Mouchoir** didn't get home over the vastly longer trip; patiently ridden, not settle fully, out wide, some headway between 3 out and 2 out, dropped away before straight. **Top Notch** was surely in the wrong Festival race but ran poorly all the same 9 weeks on from his Kempton chase win, no response as he came under pressure after 2 out. **Man of Plenty** needed more than first-time blinkers to figure at this level, predictably never landing a blow. **Coquin Mans** was well behind almost throughout. **Nautical Nitwit** was out of his depth after 10 weeks off and an overly-aggressive ride merely compounded matters; forced pace, closed down seventh, headed next, dropped away from 3 out.

CHELTENHAM Friday March 15
GOOD to SOFT

JCB Triumph Hurdle (Grade 1) (1)

Pos	Btn	Horse	Age	Wgt	Eq	Trainer	Jockey	SP
1		PENTLAND HILLS (IRE)	4	11-0		Nicky Henderson	Nico de Boinville	20/1
2	3	COEUR SUBLIME (IRE)	4	11-0		Gordon Elliott, Ireland	Davy Russell	20/1
3	3¾	GARDENS OF BABYLON (IRE)	4	11-0	(s+t)	Joseph Patrick O'Brien, Ireland	Barry Geraghty	9/1
4	3	NELSON RIVER	4	11-0		Tony Carroll	Harry Bannister	66/1
5	1	QUEL DESTIN (FR)	4	11-0		Paul Nicholls	Harry Cobden	4/1
6	1½	ECCO	4	11-0		Paul Nicholls	Harry Skelton	100/1
7	1½	ADJALI (GER)	4	11-0		Nicky Henderson	Daryl Jacob	16/1
8	1½	FRENCH MADE (FR)	4	10-7		W. P. Mullins, Ireland	P. Townend	40/1
9	nk	TIGER TAP TAP (GER)	4	11-0		W. P. Mullins, Ireland	R. Walsh	7/1
10	5	PIC D'ORHY (FR)	4	11-0	(t)	Paul Nicholls	Sam Twiston-Davies	12/1
11	5	RUNRIZED (FR)	4	11-0		W. P. Mullins, Ireland	D. J. Mullins	66/1
12	4½	HANNON (IRE)	4	11-0	(t)	John McConnell, Ireland	David Noonan	25/1
pu		AUTHORIZO (FR)	4	11-0	(t)	Gordon Elliott, Ireland	J. W. Kennedy	50/1
pu		SIR EREC (IRE)	4	11-0		Joseph Patrick O'Brien, Ireland	M. P. Walsh	11/10f

14 ran   Race Time 4m 04.80 Closing Sectional (3.70f): 53.4s (100.9%) Winning Owner: Owners Group 031

Two of the less considered runners came to the fore in a race marred by a fatal injury to the short-priced favourite Sir Erec, one of the most promising juveniles of recent seasons and a Group-class Flat horse, the form that of an average renewal, though the winner is clearly very promising to win this off just one run over hurdles, proving an able substitute for his stable-companion Fusil Raffles. **Pentland Hills** significantly up in grade, was much improved from debut, almost losing the rider at the first but otherwise showing no sign of inexperience, clearly a smart hurdling prospect; held up, travelled well, blundered first, headway after 2 out, led soon after last, stayed on well; he's open to further improvement over hurdles, and also has plenty of potential to win races back on the Flat, particularly over staying distances. **Coeur Sublime** resumed progress, faring best of those ridden prominently; prominent, travelled well, led on bridle soon after 2 out, headed soon after last, not quicken; he was raced just once on the Flat and could have even more to offer, likely to stay beyond 17f. **Gardens of Babylon** in first-time cheekpieces, wasn't in quite the same form as at Leopardstown, taking time to find full stride, the headgear not really sharpening him up; held up, effort before 2 out, not quicken entering straight, kept on well last, took third near finish. **Nelson River** outran his odds, the emphasis on stamina serving him well; in touch, shaken up 3 out, not quicken approaching last, kept on near finish; he's taken well to hurdling, though any further improvement will probably come when he is stepped up in trip. **Quel Destin** well backed, came with loads of experience and the best form among those raced in Britain, yet failed to run to his best, possibly doing a bit too much in front; led, shaken up 2 out, headed soon after, faded late on; it wouldn't be a surprise to see him bounce back at Aintree and he'll make a novice chaser at least as good in time. **Ecco** in form terms, did better with debut under belt, though this was a stern test off just one run and he was never involved; in rear, well held 2 out, kept on well straight, nearest at the finish; open to further improvement. **Adjali** ran no better than he did here on Trials day, perhaps this just not his track, his performance promising more than it delivered; waited with, travelled well, headway 3 out, challenged entering straight, weakened late on. **French Made** was asked a searching question in this grade and ran about as well as could be expected, without ever looking likely to get involved; held up, effort when not fluent 3 out, never on terms; remains with potential. **Tiger Tap Tap** had a similar chance to the third on their running at Leopardstown last time, but failed to show it, perhaps this too much of a test of stamina for him; handy, ridden 2 out, no extra run-in. **Pic d'Orhy** a leading 3-y-o hurdler in France last year, second in the Grade 1 Cambaceres when last seen, was easy to back, his stable unable to get a prep run into him, and he finished well held on first outing since leaving Francois Nicolle after 4 months off, just too buzzy in the preliminaries to do himself justice; waited with, not fluent fifth, chased leader 3 out, every chance when not fluent next, weakened entering straight; he could well prove a different proposition in time. **Runrized** was very highly tried, on just his second start over hurdles, and didn't have the experience to cope with the task; not always fluent, always behind. **Hannon** unraced on the Flat, had progressed well since starting out over hurdles, but this proved a step too far at this stage; prominent, ridden after 3 out, weakened entering straight. **Authorizo** had a fair bit to find up in grade and was effectively out of the race after the fourth; raced off the pace, hampered fourth, behind when pulled up before 2 out, reportedly had a breathing problem. **Sir Erec** so promising, met a sad end; close up when went wrong fourth, fatally injured.

Albert Bartlett Novices' Hurdle (Spa) (Grade 1) (1)

Pos	Btn	Horse	Age	Wgt	Eq	Trainer	Jockey	SP
1		MINELLA INDO (IRE)	6	11-5		Henry de Bromhead, Ireland	Rachael Blackmore	50/1
2	2	COMMANDER OF FLEET (IRE)	5	11-5		Gordon Elliott, Ireland	J. W. Kennedy	4/1f
3	7	ALLAHO (FR)	5	11-5		W. P. Mullins, Ireland	R. Walsh	8/1
4	1¾	DICKIE DIVER (IRE)	6	11-5		Nicky Henderson	Aidan Coleman	14/1
5	5	LISNAGAR OSCAR (IRE)	6	11-5		Rebecca Curtis	Sean Bowen	13/2
6	7	DERRINROSS (IRE)	8	11-5	(t)	J. P. Dempsey, Ireland	Luke Dempsey	12/1
7	¾	SALSARETTA (FR)	6	10-12		W. P. Mullins, Ireland	P. Townend	25/1
8	2	AYE AYE CHARLIE	7	11-5	(t)	Fergal O'Brien	Paddy Brennan	33/1
9	nk	CAP YORK (FR)	7	11-5		Noel Meade, Ireland	B. J. Cooper	33/1
10	nk	ASK BEN (IRE)	6	11-5		Graeme McPherson	Kielan Woods	33/1
11	4	FIRST APPROACH (IRE)	6	11-5	(s)	Noel Meade, Ireland	Sean Flanagan	25/1
12	hd	NADAITAK	5	11-5	(s)	Ben Pauling	Nico de Boinville	33/1
13	13	DORRELLS PIERJI (FR)	6	11-5		W. P. Mullins, Ireland	Noel Fehily	25/1
14	7	ROCKPOINT	6	11-5		Colin Tizzard	Tom Scudamore	33/1
pu		ALSA MIX (FR)	7	10-12	(h)	Alan King	Wayne Hutchinson	100/1
pu		BIRCHDALE (IRE)	5	11-5		Nicky Henderson	Barry Geraghty	6/1
pu		DARLAC (FR)	6	11-5	(s)	Colin Tizzard	Robbie Power	100/1
pu		DINONS (FR)	6	11-5		Gordon Elliott, Ireland	Davy Russell	9/1
pu		RHINESTONE (IRE)	6	11-5	(t)	Joseph Patrick O'Brien, Ireland	M. P. Walsh	17/2
pu		STONEY MOUNTAIN (IRE)	6	11-5		Henry Daly	Richard Johnson	16/1

20 ran   Race Time 5m 58.20   Closing Sectional (3.70f): 54.8s (100.9%)   Winning Owner: Mr Barry Maloney

The usual large field and the now fairly regular upset, the nature of the race making it susceptible to surprises, the pace and emphasis on stamina unlike anything the vast majority of these will have faced, the winner the longest priced in the race's history, though there have been 3 winners at 33/1; the form, though, should be taken at face value, the first 2 clearly strong stayers who relished the test, they along with plenty of the rest of the field likely to make an impact over fences next season. **Minella Indo** looked as if he might be overfaced, but he had clearly come on plenty for his last run and showed much improved form to get off the mark over hurdles, well served by the emphasis on stamina; prominent, tanked along, led after 3 out, stayed on strongly straight, won readily; he won't always get such a test over hurdles, but is clearly smart and could well do even better over fences, with more chances for his stamina to come into play. **Commander of Fleet** progressed again over 2f longer trip, beaten by a really stout stayer and clear of the rest; mid-division, effort before 2 out, chased leader approaching last, stayed on well; he's a smashing chasing prospect for next season, the RSA surely already in the minds of connections. **Allaho** ran creditably, though unable to confirm placings from last time with the winner, this just a very different race, the greater emphasis on stamina suiting one rather better than the other; waited with, travelled well, headway 2 out, ridden straight, no extra; he's shown himself useful in a short career over hurdles and is just the sort to do even better as a chaser next season. **Dickie Diver** upped markedly in trip, was unable to make quite the progress expected, looking short on experience when it came to the crunch, the potential there to do better, particularly once he switches to fences next season; held up, not fluent ninth, not clear run before 2 out, ran green and hung left straight, stayed on. **Lisnagar Oscar** wasn't in quite the same form as last time, though that race took several knocks in this; held up, headway before 2 out, not quicken straight. **Derrinross** after 11 weeks off, failed fully to confirm previous form, with much more competition for the lead here; led until after 3 out, weakened before last; he's a likely sort to make at least as good a chaser, though he would be coming to it rather late. **Salsaretta** was below form, reported to have post-race ataxia;

held up, took keen hold, smooth headway before 2 out, ridden straight, no extra. **Aye Aye Charlie** who'd had a breathing operation, ran his usual sort of race, though never looking likely to make much impact; in rear, still plenty to do 2 out, headway approaching last, never on terms. **Cap York** couldn't confirm the improvement shown last time, seeming to find this grade a bit too much; chased leaders, ridden before 2 out, weakened straight. **Ask Ben** had plenty on in this company; waited with, took keen hold, effort before 2 out, weakened straight; he should make at least as good a chaser next season. **First Approach** had work to do to turn the tables on the runner-up from last time, but was below form all the same, beaten by more than the longer trip; in touch, labouring approaching 2 out. **Nadaitak** faced a stiff task in this grade; prominent, ridden before ninth, weakened 2 out. **Dorrells Pierji** was not good enough for this and isn't really a thorough stayer, anyway; held up, not settle fully, effort 2 out, little impression. **Rockpoint** has had his limitations exposed since beating Lisnagar Oscar here in December and was well held in the strongest race he's contested; pressed leader, ridden before 3 out, weakened home turn. **Alsa Mix** after 11 weeks off over 3f longer trip, faced a stiff task, but failed to run her race anyway, her jumping the problem; waited with, bad mistake seventh, struggling when bad mistake 2 out, pulled up. **Birchdale** should stay this far and may have been amiss rather than beaten for stamina, so quickly was he beaten after looking a threat before the straight; in touch, travelled well, chased leaders before 2 out, weakened entering straight, eased and pulled up last; he'd looked highly promising previously and is likely to be worth another chance. **Darlac** in first-time cheekpieces, was out of his depth, this no guide to his stamina (should stay 3m); prominent, took keen hold, lost place before ninth, pulled up before last. **Dinons** ran no sort of race after 4 months off; in rear, labouring long way out, pulled up straight. **Rhinestone** was closely matched with the runner-up from last time, but didn't run his race, already in trouble when losing his action; held up, labouring eighth, pulled up 3 out; he wouldn't be sure to be suited by this sort of test, anyway. **Stoney Mountain** seemed likely to be suited by this test, but his jumping proved a serious handicap and he was beaten a long way out; handy, jumped none too fluently, took keen hold, ridden eighth, tailed off 3 out, pulled up next.

Magners Cheltenham Gold Cup Chase (Grade 1) (1)

Pos	Btn	Horse	Age	Wgt	Eq	Trainer	Jockey	SP
1		AL BOUM PHOTO (FR)	7	11-10		W. P. Mullins, Ireland	P. Townend	12/1
2	2½	ANIBALE FLY (FR)	9	11-10	(t)	A. J. Martin, Ireland	Barry Geraghty	22/1
3	3¾	BRISTOL DE MAI (FR)	8	11-10		Nigel Twiston-Davies	Daryl Jacob	18/1
4	3	NATIVE RIVER (IRE)	9	11-10	(s)	Colin Tizzard	Richard Johnson	6/1
5	1¾	CLAN DES OBEAUX (FR)	7	11-10		Paul Nicholls	Harry Cobden	5/1
6	15	ELEGANT ESCAPE (IRE)	7	11-10		Colin Tizzard	Tom O'Brien	20/1
7	3½	YALA ENKI (FR)	9	11-10		Venetia Williams	Charlie Deutsch	100/1
8	3½	PRESENTING PERCY	8	11-10	(t)	Patrick G. Kelly, Ireland	Davy Russell	10/3f
9	2¾	SHATTERED LOVE (IRE)	8	11-3	(t)	Gordon Elliott, Ireland	J. W. Kennedy	20/1
F		INVITATION ONLY (IRE)	8	11-10		W. P. Mullins, Ireland	Mr P. W. Mullins	33/1
ur		KEMBOY (FR)	7	11-10		W. P. Mullins, Ireland	D. J. Mullins	8/1
bd		DEFINITLY RED (IRE)	10	11-10		Brian Ellison	Danny Cook	50/1
pu		BELLSHILL (IRE)	9	11-10		W. P. Mullins, Ireland	R. Walsh	9/1
pu		DOUBLE SHUFFLE (IRE)	9	11-10	(h)	Tom George	Jonathan Burke	100/1
pu		MIGHT BITE (IRE)	10	11-10		Nicky Henderson	Nico de Boinville	14/1
pu		THISTLECRACK	11	11-10		Colin Tizzard	Tom Scudamore	12/1

16 ran   Race Time 6m 39.00   Closing Sectional (4.00f): 58.2s (104.2%)   Winning Owner: Mrs J. Donnelly

A deep field on paper for chasing's ultimate prize, with the principals from virtually every major 3m chase over the last year in the field, Frodon and arguably Tiger Roll notable exceptions, a wide-open race in prospect, yet there were far too many that failed to run to their best for it to be considered a great renewal, none of those at single-figure prices running their race, the favourite finishing lame, the King George winner failing to stay, last year's winner never going with the same zest, jumping frailties ending the chance of the winners of the Savills Chase and the Irish Gold Cup before the race was a third over, in addition Might Bite running as if amiss and Thistlecrack let down by jumping; the race was a bit disjointed as well, seeming well run, yet all bar Yala Enki of those still going was in contention turning for home. **Al Boum Photo** who had missed the Irish Gold Cup due to the ground, clearly relished the increased test of stamina and ran out a decisive winner, whether he had to show much in the way of improvement debatable, given how many disappointments there were behind him, though he has been beaten just once on completed starts over fences and may have still more to offer, particularly when faced with even more of a test of stamina; in rear, not always fluent, steady headway early final circuit, close up going well eighteenth, led approaching 2 out, mistake there and shaken up, kept on well, ridden out; he's young enough to make an impact in this race for a season or 2 yet, though the RSA principals look strong candidates for next season and Presenting Percy and Kemboy ought to be more serious rivals another day, even if time has passed for some of the older runners. **Anibale Fly** back at a more suitable trip, went one place better than last year, though without necessarily improving much, an element of picking up the pieces to his performance, which was strong on stamina; in rear, mistake second, reminders after and on and off the bridle subsequently, still plenty to do nineteenth, headway under pressure home turn, took second final 1f, stayed on strongly near finish; he ran well, given how wide he went, in last year's Grand National and will be a leading candidate for the race again next month. **Bristol de Mai** undoubtedly has the ability to go very close in a Gold Cup and a better round of jumping than usual enabled him to run respectably, just not so strong up the run-in as the first 2; patiently ridden, travelled well, headway eighteenth, ridden when every chance 2 out, not quicken approaching last, lost second final 1f; he's in the Grand National, set to carry top weight and not obviously well-in. **Native River** had such a demanding race when winning this so memorably last year that it may be it has impacted on his performances since, though a sluggish start immediately put him on the back foot and he had to expend energy working his way into a customary position, some effort to finish with running left in the circumstances, all under conditions less testing than suit ideally; raced lazily at start, went prominent fifth, led eleventh to fifteenth, led again seventeenth, headed approaching 2 out and outpaced, plugged on run-in. **Clan des Obeaux** was seemingly beaten for stamina after going as well as any for most of the way, certainly better than 2 of the 4 that beat him; in touch, travelled well, tracked pace early final circuit, shaken up entering straight, every chance when not fluent 2 out, weakened run-in; his King George form obviously took some knocks here, but there's every chance that he will bounce back quickly. **Elegant Escape** had made good progress this season, but he ideally needs more of a test of stamina; chased leaders, outpaced eighteenth, in touch entering straight, mistake 2 out, weakened; he holds a Grand National entry, on the young side for that race, though the emphasis on stamina would be right up his street. **Yala Enki** is a very smart handicapper on his day, but this company proved beyond him; in touch, labouring fourteenth, tailed off when hampered approaching 2 out. **Presenting Percy** was sent off favourite, despite not having run over fences since winning the RSA Chase at last year's Festival, and clearly didn't run up to expectations, on his toes in the preliminaries and never going with his customary verve; held up, not always fluent, never travelling well, effort nineteenth, weakened approaching 2 out, lame, saddle also reportedly slipped; he would have beaten the winner in the RSA last year had that one completed, and he clearly has the ability to figure at this level in future, if all is well. **Shattered Love** last year's Golden Miller winner, had had a breathing operation since her poor run at Christmas, but failed to take the eye beforehand and was again well held; in rear, ridden fifteenth, some headway eighteenth, in touch entering straight, weakened, dismounted, reportedly suffered post-race ataxia; she holds a Grand National entry, but it is hard to make a case for her at present. **Invitation Only** led until eighth, fell tenth, dead. **Kemboy** had his winning run ended almost before the race had begun; held up, landed very awkwardly and unseated rider first. **Definitly Red** had made little impact in 4 previous Festival visits, but didn't get the chance to improve that record; prominent, brought down tenth. **Bellshill** had jumped well when winning in a small field at Leopardstown but, much more patiently ridden, made 3 bad errors in the first mile, his rider having little option but to call it a day; held up, bad mistake fifth, blundered seventh, eighth, pulled up. **Double Shuffle** has only one piece of form that entitles him to a ticket to this event, no sign of him showing that level here; in touch, labouring fourteenth, pulled up before eighteenth. **Might Bite** last year's runner-up, had reportedly had a breathing operation and been treated for ulcers since the King George, but some problem persists as he cut out entirely entering the straight after helping force the pace, having not jumped so well as usual; pressed leader, not always fluent, travelled well, led eighth until eleventh, led fifteenth, sixteenth, folded tamely entering straight, pulled up before 2 out; he reportedly may drop in trip, but it's hard to see that as the answer to his problems. **Thistlecrack** ran no sort of race, primarily due to his jumping letting him down; held up, jumped poorly, labouring badly approaching halfway, tailed off sixteenth, pulled up.

AINTREE Thursday April 4
GOOD to SOFT

Betway Bowl Chase (Grade 1) (1)

Pos	Btn	Horse	Age	Wgt	Eq	Trainer	Jockey	SP
1		KEMBOY (FR)	7	11-7		W. P. Mullins, Ireland	R. Walsh	9/4F
2	9	CLAN DES OBEAUX (FR)	7	11-7		Paul Nicholls	Harry Cobden	11/4
3	hd	BALKO DES FLOS (FR)	8	11-7		Henry de Bromhead, Ireland	Rachael Blackmore	20/1
4	1	BRISTOL DE MAI (FR)	8	11-7		Nigel Twiston-Davies	Daryl Jacob	7/2
5	5	ROAD TO RESPECT (IRE)	8	11-7		Noel Meade, Ireland	Sean Flanagan	9/2
6	40	ELEGANT ESCAPE (IRE)	7	11-7		Colin Tizzard	Tom O'Brien	10/1

6 ran Race Time 6m 35.20 Closing Sectional (3.15f): 46.3s (107.8%) Winning Owner: Supreme Racing/Brett Graham/Ken Sharp

Minor roles in either the Ryanair or Gold Cup were the best this field could boast from Cheltenham yet from it emerged a relative youngster with a valid claim to top spot in the staying division, Kemboy's jumping letting him down at Cheltenham but giving him the edge in this as he produced a performance right up there with what it had taken his stablemate Al Boum Photo to land the latter prize, Mullins going from seeking a first Gold

Cup win to trainer of arguably the 2 premier horses on the staying chase scene within 3 weeks; the winner had the advantage of dictating a modest pace, best placed to strike as it finally developed 2 out, but his dominance was such that he'd almost certainly have prevailed with comfort under any tactical circumstances. **Kemboy** put his Gold Cup blip immediately behind him, avoiding the sort of hard race others had endured at Cheltenham due to his early departure there but, more significantly, setting himself apart in terms of ability, revealing that bit more each time he's made the track during a sequence of 5 successive wins when completing that has thrust him unerringly into the upper echelons, jumping issues that had held him back on both previous visits to chases on these shores erased from memory; soon in front, controlling matters, he jumped best (if slightly to the right) and was still going powerfully as it took shape from 2 out, sprinting away on the flat in a style rarely seen in the staying chase ranks, undeniably impressive dominance for all he'd had the run of things; there wasn't much between him and stablemate Al Boum Photo in the market on the off in the Gold Cup, and that near-parity can't help but be reflected in their ratings after the 2 major spring festivals, the pair still mere 7-y-os and in the very best hands to boot, an ominous sign for the largely older, less progressive crowd outside Mullins' yard, though the addition of RSA 1-2 Topofthegame and Santini—not to mention the following day's Grade 1 novice winner Lostintranslation—into the mix next season suggests they won't have it all their own way, 2019/20 a potentially stellar one in the staying division. **Clan des Obeaux** has seen his rise halted at the spring festivals but excuses haven't been too hard to find, with the effects of a Gold Cup that stretched his stamina probably partly to blame for this rather underwhelming bid at redemption in the face of a more suitable test, also leaving the impression a truer gallop would have shown him to better advantage; there are holes to be picked in his King George success, but he'd also shaped like a top-class operator for most of the Gold Cup and, in coming under pressure early in the straight (before the others in the frame) 3 weeks on, he gave the impression he wasn't at the top of his game, even wandering for good measure under firmer handling between 3 out and 2 out, testament to his resolution that he was able to take advantage of the mistake of Balko des Flos to get past that rival for a remote second. **Balko des Flos** revived 3 weeks later than might have been expected, a return to the Ryanair doing little to stimulate him but this tactical affair over further prompting a season's best, cost second by a blunder at the last after he'd kept tabs on Kemboy for longest as the race developed in the straight, 2 lengths clear of Clan des Obeaux and keeping on fine at the time of his error; it remains to be seen whether this proves a false dawn, however. **Bristol de Mai** found standards slipping again after a Gold Cup performance that had perhaps suggested he'd turned over a new leaf for good, like Clan des Obeaux probably unsuited by the relative emphasis on speed just 3 weeks after a hard race, though his jumping flaws also resurfaced (hit seventh and 4 out), decidedly one paced when speed was required on the run from 2 out, as though Cheltenham had indeed taken the edge off him; on the plus side, he'll be fresh again when bidding to become the first horse to win 3 successive Betfair Chases in the autumn. **Road To Respect** was found wanting (not for the first time) back over a staying trip but was probably undone by more than a test that stretched his stamina, shaken up to keep tabs even before the pace lifted and soon flattening out following a brief surge around the field into a threatening position 2 out, as much as any leaving the impression this came too soon after a hard race at Cheltenham. **Elegant Escape** regularly takes some driving but was particularly lacklustre 3 weeks on from the Gold Cup, baulked at the first, making mistakes after and never going well from the fourth, labouring badly before 4 out; his yard hasn't had quite the season that might have been expected, Elegant Escape one of the success stories but perhaps over the top by now.

Betway Aintree Hurdle (Grade 1) (1)

Pos	Btn	Horse	Age	Wgt	Eq	Trainer	Jockey	SP
1		SUPASUNDAE	9	11-7	(t)	Mrs J. Harrington, Ireland	Robbie Power	15/2
2	1¼	BUVEUR D'AIR (FR)	8	11-7		Nicky Henderson	Barry Geraghty	5/6f
3	½	CH'TIBELLO (FR)	8	11-7		Dan Skelton	Harry Skelton	14/1
4	31	SUMMERVILLE BOY (IRE)	7	11-7		Tom George	Jonathan Burke	25/1
5	10	SILVER STREAK (IRE)	6	11-7		Evan Williams	Adam Wedge	25/1
F		MELON	7	11-7	(s)	W. P. Mullins, Ireland	P. Townend	8/1
pu		FAUGHEEN (IRE)	11	11-7		W. P. Mullins, Ireland	R. Walsh	4/1

7 ran   Race Time 5m 09.10   Closing Sectional (3.15f): 52.3s (93.1%)   Winning Owner: Ann & Alan Potts Limited

A fascinating race in anticipation, though not necessarily a strong one, largely because most had questions to answer, primarily about stamina, but also in some cases about well-being, plenty failing to give their running and enough known about the winner and the third to think a relatively cautious view of the form is desirable, the race developing into quite a slog in foul conditions. **Supasundae** wasted no time getting back to form back down in trip, running his best race of the season, though likely to have found the runner-up below form rather than to have improved significantly himself; in touch, headway under pressure eighth, left in front 3 out, kept on well run-in, asserted final 50 yds. **Buveur d'Air** couldn't quite get back to his best after his mishap at Cheltenham, back up in trip for a race he'd won in 2017, his season something of an anticlimax after the style of his win at Newcastle had promised so much; tracked pace until fifth, effort when hampered 3 out, ridden soon after, every chance last, held final 50 yds. **Ch'tibello** back up in trip, ran well upped in grade, clearly back in good heart after his breathing operation; held up, travelled well, took closer order straight, challenged from 3 out, switched run-in, no extra final 100 yds. **Summerville Boy** upped in trip (bred to stay), had been found to have a hairline fracture after his last run, but fared no better after 4 months off; held up, took keen hold, not fluent fourth, bad mistake seventh, labouring next; his season has been a write-off. **Silver Streak** upped in trip, seemed an unlikely stayer, but he just didn't run his race, beaten well before stamina came into play, perhaps his big effort at Cheltenham having left its mark; dropped out, ridden before 3 out, left behind after. **Melon** upped in trip, was far from certain to stay and, though still in front when he departed, the likelihood is that he would have finished well held; handy, not settle fully, led circuit out, clear soon after, hung right, reduced advantage entering straight, fell 3 out. **Faugheen** was amiss, reported to have had a fibrillating heart; led, faltered after fifth, headed soon after, pulled up before next; he's been a tremendous servant over the years and hopefully will have the chance to end his career on a higher note at Punchestown.

AINTREE Friday April 5
GOOD to SOFT

Betway Mildmay Novices' Chase (Grade 1) (1)

Pos	Btn	Horse	Age	Wgt	Eq	Trainer	Jockey	SP
1		LOSTINTRANSLATION (IRE)	7	11-4		Colin Tizzard	Robbie Power	3/1
2	6	TOPOFTHEGAME (IRE)	7	11-4	(t)	Paul Nicholls	Harry Cobden	10/11f
3	½	TOP VILLE BEN (IRE)	7	11-4	(h)	Philip Kirby	Sean Quinlan	14/1
4	7	MR WHIPPED (IRE)	6	11-4	(s)	Nicky Henderson	Nico de Boinville	11/1
5	12	CHRIS'S DREAM (IRE)	7	11-4		Henry de Bromhead, Ireland	Rachael Blackmore	5/1
F		CRUCIAL ROLE	7	11-4		Dan Skelton	Harry Skelton	28/1

6 ran Race Time 6m 31.80 Closing Sectional (3.15f): 48.7s (101.6%) Winning Owner: Taylor & O'Dwyer

With Topofthegame not in the same form as when winning at Cheltenham, this probably isn't that strong a piece of form for a Grade 1, but there was a lot to like about the winner on his first start at 3m+ and he'll be a serious contender against the principals from the RSA even when they are on song; the third was allowed an easy lead and the race developed only really from 3 out. **Lostintranslation** upped in trip, made it third time lucky in Grade 1 novices, no Defi du Seuil in opposition this time, not needing to improve with the favourite below form, but still with a lot to like about the style of his win; in touch, jumped well, travelled strongly, smooth headway entering straight, led 2 out, steadied into last, shaken up run-in, impressive; he is sure to progress further next season, with the Ladbrokes Trophy an obvious starting point, further increase in emphasis on stamina sure to be to his advantage. **Topofthegame** patently wasn't in the same form as at Cheltenham, falling into second after looking in trouble a fair way out, this probably coming too soon for one who has been sparingly raced until now; patiently ridden, not fluent fourteenth, ridden after, faltered 3 out, rallied run-in, took second close home; he'll likely bounce back when fresh next season. **Top Ville Ben** showed improved form back in graded company, though he was seen to maximum advantage, despite, oddly, tending to go right (had jumped left when going right handed at Ascot); allowed soft lead, ridden after 3 out, headed 2 out, not quicken last, lost second close home; this won't have done much for his prospective mark, though big handicaps are his likely destination, a National of some description likely to be on the agenda next season. **Mr Whipped** upped in trip, in first-time cheekpieces after 4 months off, failed to progress as anticipated, perhaps needing a stronger gallop to be seen to advantage; patiently ridden, not fluent twelfth, mistake 4 out, left behind approaching 2 out; he remains with potential after just 3 runs over fences. **Chris's Dream** was well held, his jumping not up to scratch in this grade, though he shaped as if amiss in the end; held up, jumped none too fluently, effort when blundered 3 out, stopped quickly; he had looked promising prior to this and may well progress further back in calmer waters. **Crucial Role** met a sad end; chased leader, still handy when fell fatally 3 out.

JLT Chase (Melling) (Grade 1) (1)

Pos	Btn	Horse	Age	Wgt	Eq	Trainer	Jockey	SP
1		MIN (FR)	8	11-7		W. P. Mullins, Ireland	R. Walsh	2/1f
2	20	POLITOLOGUE (FR)	8	11-7	(h+t)	Paul Nicholls	Harry Cobden	5/2
3	9	WAITING PATIENTLY (IRE)	8	11-7	(s)	Ruth Jefferson	Brian Hughes	9/4
4	10	HELL'S KITCHEN	8	11-7	(h+t)	Harry Fry	Barry Geraghty	14/1
5	12	GOD'S OWN (IRE)	11	11-7		Tom George	Paddy Brennan	25/1
pu		TOP NOTCH (FR)	8	11-7		Nicky Henderson	Daryl Jacob	8/1

6 ran Race Time 5m 03.40 Closing Sectional (3.15f): 47.0s (102.1%) Winning Owner: Mrs S. Ricci

No Altior or Cyrname, or any representative from the Ryanair at Cheltenham, but the 2019 Melling Chase still brought together 3 top-class chasers and will be remembered as quite possibly the crowning moment of Min's career as he surpassed the aforementioned Cyrname's Ascot Chase demolition both in terms of winning margin and, most likely, form—even a conservative view of this sees him running to a mark in the mid-170s; there was plenty of chopping and changing for second place without anything going as far as taking the winner on in front, though that's not to say the pace wasn't an end-to-end one. **Min** with plenty of confidence behind him in the market, not only banished the memories of his subdued showing in the Champion Chase but proved better than ever as he put up a performance every bit as authoritative—indeed possibly even more so—as Cyrname in the Ascot Chase, handing out a very similar beating to Politologue and a bigger one to Waiting Patiently, the return to front-running seeming very much in his favour (usual earplugs left out); he had various pursuers but jumped boldly in front, gained a couple of lengths on his rivals under a motionless Walsh at the third last, easily drew clear from the next and was already in full control when measuring the last superbly; with Altior and Cyrname set to clash at Sandown, Min should have the Punchestown Champion Chase at his mercy, while connections will no doubt be eyeing another crack at Altior next season on the back of this. **Politologue** back up in trip, had edged out Min to win this last year but had little hope of containing him this time given the brilliance of that one's performance, the effort of giving chase seeming to tell (was said to have bled); chased leader until fourth, allowed to slide back to fourth at the seventh, went second again 3 out but was left behind by the winner from the next. **Waiting Patiently** began the season with so much potential (sent off just 4/1 for the King George on his reappearance) but, though unlucky that day, hasn't got close to the form of his listed win at Kempton last season—let alone his Ascot Chase performance—in 2 subsequent outings this campaign, the application of first-time cheekpieces failing to produce the desired spark; typically waited with, his rider gave him a slap down the neck after the ninth and, though he made ground out wide 4 out, he wasn't fluent either there or the next and couldn't make any further impression, disappointingly readily seen off by Politologue for second. **Hell's Kitchen** back up in trip, again looked comfortable at this level for a long way but found his jumping letting him down in the second half of the race; settled in touch, he went second before the eighth but made a bad mistake at the eleventh, already on the retreat when not fluent 4 out and held when steadied into 2 out. **God's Own** won this race in 2016 but his best days are surely behind him now and was well below form, perhaps something of a rush to get him back after being struck into at Cheltenham; patiently ridden, untidy eighth, effort approaching home turn, held when steadied into 2 out. **Top Notch** again ran poorly back over fences, probably more to it than just a fairly shoddy round of jumping; mid-division, untidy first, chased leader briefly from fourth, blundered eighth, lost place and shaken up circuit out, lost further ground eleventh, reminders after, weakening when clouted 4 out, pulled up; he has something to prove now, though the Oaksey Chase at Sandown that he won last year would give him a platform to do so.

Doom Bar Sefton Novices' Hurdle (Grade 1) (1)

Pos	Btn	Horse	Age	Wgt	Eq	Trainer	Jockey	SP
1		CHAMP (IRE)	7	11-4		Nicky Henderson	M. P. Walsh	9/4f
2	3	EMITOM (IRE)	5	11-4		Warren Greatrex	Gavin Sheehan	5/1
3	7	LISNAGAR OSCAR (IRE)	6	11-4		Rebecca Curtis	Sean Bowen	11/2
4	2¾	WALK AWAY (IRE)	6	11-4		Henry de Bromhead, Ireland	Robbie Power	12/1
5	3¼	ARTHUR MAC (IRE)	6	11-4		Henry Oliver	Liam Heard	50/1
6	3¾	CHAMPAGNE WELL (IRE)	6	11-4		Fergal O'Brien	Paddy Brennan	25/1
7	19	DOWNTOWN GETAWAY (IRE)	6	11-4		Nicky Henderson	Nico de Boinville	8/1
8	hd	ARDLETHEN (IRE)	6	11-4		Dan Skelton	Harry Skelton	16/1
9	½	KINGSPLACE (IRE)	7	11-4		Nigel Twiston-Davies	Sam Twiston-Davies	66/1
10	2¾	TREVELYN'S CORN (IRE)	6	11-4	(t)	Paul Nicholls	Harry Cobden	18/1
11	7	DALLAS DES PICTONS (FR)	6	11-4		Gordon Elliott, Ireland	J. W. Kennedy	4/1
pu		THE CAPTAINS INN (IRE)	5	11-4		Ben Pauling	Daryl Jacob	33/1

12 ran   Race Time 6m 17.80   Closing Sectional (3.15f): 46.5s (103.7%)   Winning Owner: Mr John P. McManus

Not the test of stamina this race is designed to be, with the pace steady for much of the way, all bar Kingsplace of those remaining closely grouped 3 out, that the field became so well strung out in the closing stages testament to the winner's class, though also to the standard of jumping, which was lacking somewhat, and the failure to settle of several. **Champ** recorded a second Grade 1 success, lots to like about the way he went about things, the manner he saw out the trip opening up plenty of opportunities for chasing next season; held up, travelled well, mistake seventh, smooth headway straight, led on bridle 2 out, ridden after last, kept on well; likely to make a leading novice over fences. **Emitom** lost his unbeaten record, but acquitted himself well up in grade, likely to have been further clear of the third had the cards fallen more kindly; dropped out, not settle fully, headway when short of room after 3 out, shaken up after next, mistake last, chased leader run-in, kept on well; he had no problem with the markedly longer trip and is open to further improvement, like so many a prospective novice chaser for next season. **Lisnagar Oscar** ran a shade better than in the Spa, though his last 2 runs have perhaps suggested his limitations as a novice hurdler; virtually upsides leader, jumped on eighth, headed 2 out, no extra approaching final 1f. **Walk Away** up in grade, built on debut promise, despite his lack of experience showing; in rear, not always fluent, travelled smoothly, headway after 3 out, fourth when mistake last, one paced; open to further improvement. **Arthur Mac** upped in trip, seemed to excel himself in this stronger company; in touch, effort when blundered 3 out, lost place, kept on again run-in. **Champagne Well** back up in trip, ran about as well as could have been expected upped in grade; tracked pace, blundered third, lost place fifth, headway before 3 out, challenged between last 2, no extra; he's very much the type to make a chaser, a useful one at least. **Downtown Getaway** upped in trip/class, was well held after 11 weeks off, ruining his chance by failing to settle; in touch, pulled way into prominent position fourth, shaken up after 3 out, soon done with; he may yet do better back in calmer waters though, like so many of these, his future lies over fences. **Ardlethen** was well held up in grade; waited with, headway before 3 out, ridden approaching 2 out, weakened after, eased run-in. **Kingsplace** faced a stiff task in this grade, the only one out of contention 3 out; close up, ridden after 4 out, lost place quickly straight. **Trevelyn's Corn** upped in trip, was found wanting at this higher level, too much for him at this stage of his career; led, took keen hold, mistake eighth, headed, every chance still 3 out, bad mistake next, behind when hit last; he's a chaser on looks. **Dallas des Pictons** is best not judged on this run; in touch, took closer order sixth, every chance straight, ridden 2 out, found little, beaten when mistake last, heavily eased off (reportedly lost action); looks very much the part for chasing. **The Captains Inn** upped in trip and grade, didn't get the chance to show what he could do; held up, took keen hold, mistake tenth, badly hampered soon after, pulled up.

AINTREE Saturday April 6
GOOD

Doom Bar Maghull Novices' Chase (Grade 1) (1)

Pos	Btn	Horse	Age	Wgt	Eq	Trainer	Jockey	SP
1		ORNUA (IRE)	8	11-4		Henry de Bromhead, Ireland	Davy Russell	3/1jf
2	1¾	US AND THEM (IRE)	6	11-4	(t)	Joseph Patrick O'Brien, Ireland	J. J. Slevin	3/1jf
3	1¼	DESTRIER (FR)	6	11-4		Dan Skelton	Harry Skelton	7/1
4	20	CLONDAW CASTLE (IRE)	7	11-4		Tom George	Ciaran Gethings	13/2
5	nk	KNOCKNANUSS (IRE)	9	11-4		Gary Moore	Jamie Moore	8/1
6	1	LALOR (GER)	7	11-4		Kayley Woollacott	Richard Johnson	7/2
7	25	CAID DU LIN (FR)	7	11-4	(b+t)	Dr Richard Newland	Sam Twiston-Davies	20/1

7 ran Race Time 3m 50.80 Closing Sectional (3.15f): 45.6s (100.9%) Winning Owner: John J Phelan/Syed Momin

Five of the 7 had contested the Arkle last time out, including the second, fourth and fifth from that contest, the market finding it hard to choose between the runner-up and the 2 non-finishers from the race, the field closely matched on paper, with just 6 lb between all the runners on Timeform ratings, the winner finding a little improvement under a canny ride, the race well run, though not overly so. **Ornua** proved at least as good as ever, gaining compensation for his mishap in the Arkle under a well-judged ride, controlling a race in which there had looked potential for quite a bit of competition for the lead; led, jumped well, went with zest, quickened after 3 out, ridden run-in, ran on; he's likely to be aimed at the Tingle Creek, but would need to improve a stone to be involved in an average running, never mind one involving potentially any of Altior, Cyrname or Min. **Us And Them** back under a more usual ride, matched his best form, but had to settle for second for the fifth start running (last 4 in Grade 1s), sticking to his task after looking a little short of pace; prominent, not fluent fifth, second when mistake 3 out, kept on run-in, took second final 100 yds. **Destrier** ran well upped in grade, the least experienced of these over fences; held up, travelled well, mistake third, good progress 4 out, chased leader approaching 2 out, shaken up after, kept on but no impression on winner, lost second final 100 yds; he could well make an impact in good 2m handicaps next season. **Clondaw Castle** was well below the form he showed in the Arkle, typically travelling smoothly but folding even more alarmingly than he had at Cheltenham; in touch, jumped well in main, travelled well, yet to be asked for effort when not fluent 2 out, shaken up and found nothing. **Knocknanuss** was well held, not helping himself with the way he raced, his jumping not inspiring confidence either; chased leader, not always fluent, pulled hard, lost place eighth, blundered 4 out, labouring after; he'll have a bit to prove when next seen. **Lalor** shaped a bit better than in the Arkle, but he again left the impression all wasn't well; waited with, blundered seventh, soon done with, hit 3 out, not persevered with once held; his season has obviously failed to deliver on the great things expected. **Caid du Lin** up in grade, found this a struggle, virtually from the off; in rear, slow and right first and second and reminders, always behind.

TIMEFORM'S BEST OF 2018/19

The most popular result of the season was undoubtedly that of Tiger Roll in the Grand National, with Gordon Elliott's charge sparking frenzied scenes at Aintree by becoming the first horse since Red Rum to win consecutive renewals of the race. Tiger Roll had earlier won his second Cross Country Chase at the Cheltenham Festival to join a select group of horses with four Festival wins, one that also now includes Altior after his second victory in the Queen Mother Champion Chase earlier that afternoon. Top two-mile chasers often struggle for wider recognition compared to Grand National heroes, but Altior now joins Istabraq and Kauto Star in Timeform's pantheon of three-times Horse of the Year award winners. Tiger Roll and Altior aside, perhaps the best advertisement for National Hunt racing came on the Thursday of the Cheltenham Festival, when Ryanair Chase winner Frodon and Stayers' Hurdle hero Paisley Park provided two of the human stories of the jumping year. The latter has the potential to dominate his division for many years to come, while Frodon—along with Clan des Obeaux and Cyrname—formed a trio of Grade 1-winning chasers who helped Paul Nicholls to regain the trainers' championship for the first time since 2015/16. Over in Ireland, Willie Mullins was crowned champion trainer for the twelfth year in succession, seeing off the challenge of Elliott much more comfortably than in recent seasons, and the Closutton maestro will have been particularly satisfied to be able to tick off two of the major omissions from his outstanding CV, with Al Boum Photo and Burrows Saint winning the Cheltenham Gold Cup and Irish Grand National, respectively.

Staying chasers

The prolonged dry spell during the opening stages of the season ensured that **Al Boum Photo** (c174) didn't make his reappearance until New Year's Day—when comfortably winning a listed heat at Tramore—and he was overlooked in the Gold Cup by Ruby Walsh, who chose to ride the previous month's Irish Gold Cup winner **Bellshill** (c165) instead. In the event, however, Paul Townend never had a moment's worry, always in the right place on Al Boum Photo, who stayed on strongly on the run-in to beat the previous year's third **Anibale Fly** (c167) by two and a half lengths, with dual Betfair Chase winner **Bristol de Mai** (c169x) another three and three quarter lengths back in third. 2018 hero **Native River** (c165+) never looked comfortable when fourth in the defence of his Cheltenham crown, while arguably the biggest disappointment of the race was **Presenting Percy** (c165+) in eighth; he had a far from ideal preparation, however, with the Gold Cup being his first start over fences since winning the RSA at the previous year's Festival, and there is no doubt that he has the ability to figure at the top level in the future, if all is well after reportedly finishing lame at Prestbury Park. For his part, Al Boum Photo is still young enough to make his presence felt in the blue riband for a season or two yet, though he wasn't even the top-rated staying chaser in his own yard by the end of the campaign, with that honour instead

Kemboy puts Al Boum Photo to the sword in the Punchestown Gold Cup

belonging to **Kemboy** (c176). An early casualty at Cheltenham, that was the only glitch in his campaign, with his wins including the Savills Chase at Leopardstown (by seven and a half lengths from **Monalee** (c165)), the Bowl Chase at Aintree (by nine lengths from King George winner **Clan des Obeaux** (c166)) and the Punchestown Gold Cup, when beating Al Boum Photo by two lengths under Ruby Walsh, who promptly hung up his riding boots in the aftermath. Kemboy deserves to be viewed as the best staying chaser around on the back of that effort and rightly heads the ante-post market for the 2020 Gold Cup at around 6/1. The likely campaign for **Tiger Roll** (c167) this season is much less certain at this stage, with owner Michael O'Leary reluctant to commit to a third Grand National tilt, but he has a rating that suggests he would be capable of mixing it with the best staying chasers around if asked to do so, while **Frodon** (c167) was considered strongly for the most recent renewal of the Gold Cup after beating Welsh National winner **Elegant Escape** (c161) in the Cotswold Chase on Trials Day. Ultimately, connections settled on the Ryanair Chase as his Festival target, and they were rewarded with a typically game performance to defeat **Aso** (c166) and **Road To Respect** (c165), making Bryony Frost the first female jockey to ride a Grade 1 winner over jumps at the meeting.

Two-mile chasers

The five wins that **Altior** (c180p) recorded in 2018/19 ensured that he broke the record of another former Timeform Horse of the Year, Big Buck's, by extending his unbeaten sequence over jumps to 19 races. Admittedly, he did get a brief fright when joined by **Politologue** (c166) and **Sceau Royal** (c164) at the final fence in the Champion Chase, but there was still a sense of inevitability about the way that he rallied on the run-in, typically finding plenty up the hill to assert. Last seen making the most of a good opportunity in the Celebration Chase at Sandown, his strength at the finish of his races suggests that he'll get further—an option that his connections are reportedly keen to explore this season—but he's by no means a certainty on pedigree to stay 3m if heading to the King George, while that division is also much deeper than the one he has dominated for the last few seasons. Of the rest, **Min** (c174) won the John Durkan Chase and Dublin Chase—in which 2017 Champion Chase winner **Special Tiara** (c152) sadly lost his life—on his first two starts, and, having had an off-day when only fifth in the Champion Chase, he then proved better than ever to win the Melling Chase at Aintree (by 20 lengths from Politologue), surging clear under a motionless Ruby Walsh. Unsurprisingly, Willie Mullins' charge still looked to be feeling the effects of that big effort when only fourth behind stablemate **Un de Sceaux** (c170) in the Champion Chase at Punchestown 25 days later, and with Altior set to go up in trip, there should be more races to be won with him in this division in 2019/20. Similar comments apply to **Cyrname** (c173+), who wasn't seen on the track after a most impressive victory in the Ascot Chase (by 17 lengths from **Waiting Patiently** (c164+)) in February, with a potential clash with Altior at Sandown being ruled out on account of the ground being faster than ideal. With his best form to date having come over intermediate trips, he is another who is not short of options this season, while it will be interesting to see how much life there still is in the popular veterans **Simply Ned** (c162) and Un de Sceaux, both Grade 1 winners at two miles during the latest campaign who will turn 13 and 12, respectively, when 2020 comes around.

Altior extends his winning sequence over jumps to 19 at Sandown

Novice chasers

We had to wait until the penultimate day of the Irish National Hunt season for the leading novice chaser to announce his arrival on the big stage, with the lightly-raced **Chacun Pour Soi** (c169p) producing a top-class performance to win the Ryanair Novices' Chase at the Punchestown Festival. Making only his second start for Willie Mullins, he coped easily with the step up in class to dent a couple of big reputations, beating JLT winner **Defi du Seuil** (c164p) by four and a quarter lengths, with his Grade 1-winning stablemates **Duc des Genievres** (c162+) and **Voix du Reve** (c156+) both out with the washing in third and fourth, respectively. It was hard not to be impressed with the winner and the sky is very much the limit if he can stand more regular racing in 2019/20. A key feature of the latest season was the ongoing rivalry between Defi du Seuil and **Lostintranslation** (c160p), one that the former got the best of more often than not. Colin Tizzard's charge enjoyed his day in the sun, though, when winning the Mildmay Novices' Chase at Aintree (by six lengths from RSA winner **Topofthegame** (c162p)), and he looks sure to progress further this season, especially when the emphasis is even more on stamina. As for Topofthegame, the sad news came through in September that he had been ruled out of the 2019/20 campaign due to injury, but his form is still likely to be well advertised by the likes of **Santini** (c161p) and **Delta Work** (c163p)—a wide-margin winner at Punchestown subsequently—the pair who chased him home in what looked one of the strongest renewals of the RSA in recent memory; that pair both remain with potential and should develop into major contenders for top honours in staying chases this season. Similar comments apply to the dual Grade 1-winning mare **La Bague Au Roi** (c151p), who wasn't at the top of her game when chasing home **Kalashnikov** (c154p) in the Manifesto Novices' Chase at Aintree on her final start. Others to taste success at Grade 1 level in this division included **Dynamite Dollars** (c153+) and **Le Richebourg** (c158p), both of whom were ruled out of the major spring festivals through injury, while **A Plus Tard** (c157), **Burrows Saint** (c155) and **Talkischeap** (c155) all achieved notable ratings in winning major handicaps, the first-named when streaking clear to provide Rachael Blackmore with a first Cheltenham Festival success in the Close Brothers Novices' Handicap Chase.

Staying hurdlers

Few could have anticipated the giant strides that **Paisley Park** (h166p) made as a staying hurdler, quickly improving from handicaps to becoming a potentially dominant figure in this division for years to come. His *pièce de résistance* came when extending his winning run to five in the Stayers' Hurdle at Cheltenham, surging to the front on the approach to the last, having turned into the straight around seven lengths down with as many rivals ahead of him. Still only a seven-year-old, there should be plenty of big days left in Paisley Park yet. **Sam Spinner** (h158) produced his best effort of the season when filling the runner-up spot at Cheltenham, with the Rich Ricci-owned pair of **Faugheen** (h154) and **Bapaume** (h156) doing best of the Irish in third and fourth, respectively. Surprisingly, Ricci left the Cheltenham Festival empty-handed for the first time since 2011, but the disappointment of seeing **Benie des Dieux** (h159) fall when clear at the final flight of the Mares' Hurdle was compensated for to some extent by her subsequent exploits, with his star mare showing no ill effects from that tumble with wins in the Mares Champion Hurdle at Punchestown and the Grande Course de Haies d'Auteuil. **Presenting Percy** (h160+) and **Tiger Roll** (h154)—both of whom are better known for their exploits in staying chases—each make their second appearance in these pages, having won graded hurdles as part of their preparations for Cheltenham, while it was a pair of horses trained by Harry Fry who ruled in the absence of Paisley Park at Aintree and Punchestown. **If The Cap Fits** (h159+) got the ball rolling when beating Mares' Hurdle winner **Roksana** (h149)—the main beneficiary of Benie des Dieux's fall—in a photo finish to the Liverpool Hurdle, and three weeks later it was the turn of **Unowhatimeanharry** (h151), who bounced back to form from out of the blue to spring a 16/1-shock in the Champion Stayers Hurdle at Punchestown.

Two-mile hurdlers

The Champion Hurdle was one of the most highly-anticipated for many years, with the talented mares **Apple's Jade** (h162) and **Laurina** (h154) looking to pose a serious threat to **Buveur d'Air** (h163), who was attempting to emulate some legendary names by winning the race for a third year in succession. The odds on none of that trio making the places would have been sizeable to say the least, but that was ultimately what transpired, with the reigning champion falling at an early stage and the two mares both running well below their best. Apple's Jade had been unstoppable in the build-up to Cheltenham, winning all four starts by an aggregate of 73 lengths, but she was never travelling as well as usual on the day and ultimately trailed in a well-held sixth, with the honours instead going to **Espoir d'Allen** (h170), the first five-year-old to win the race since Katchit in 2008. Even with the disappointments in behind taken into account, it was hard not to be impressed by the manner of his performance, beating the previous year's runner-up **Melon** (h155x)

The ill-fated Espoir d'Allen on his way to Champion Hurdle glory

and the very smart **Silver Streak** (h154) by 15 lengths, the widest winning margin in the race's history. A landmark success for trainer Gavin Cromwell, Espoir d'Allen looked set to be a major force in this division, but sadly it was not to be; he had to be put down in August after suffering an injury in a freak accident at Cromwell's yard. Buveur d'Air quickly got his career back on track after his Cheltenham blip, finishing a brave second to **Supasundae** (h157) in the Aintree Hurdle, before reversing the places with that rival to land a stylish success in the Punchestown Champion Hurdle. **Sharjah** (h157+), who was brought down by Buveur d'Air's fall at Cheltenham, was one of this division's star performers in the first half of the season with ready wins in the Morgiana Hurdle at Punchestown and Ryanair Hurdle at Leopardstown, while **Verdana Blue** (h159) is another who showed herself to be a very smart performer when getting her favoured fast conditions, claiming the notable scalp of stablemate Buveur d'Air in the Christmas Hurdle at Kempton on Boxing Day, before defying a BHA mark of 154 to land the Scottish Champion Hurdle at Ayr on her final start.

Novice hurdlers

Top honours in this division went to **Klassical Dream** (h157p), who will forever be the answer to the quiz question *'which was Ruby Walsh's final Cheltenham Festival winner?'*. That is unlikely to be the only thing that he is remembered for, however, with the manner of his final two wins—in the Supreme Novices' Hurdle at Cheltenham and Champion Novices' Hurdle at Punchestown—suggesting that he has all the necessary tools to be a big player in open Grade 1 company this season, with the Champion Hurdle reported to be his main target. **Felix Desjy** (h146) was comfortably put in his place by Klassical Dream at Punchestown, but there was plenty to like about his earlier win in the Top Novices' Hurdle at Aintree, when beating the consistent **Aramon** (h145) by a length and a half, and he has the makings of a smart novice chaser in 2019/20, a comment that also applies to the Olly Murphy-trained pair of **Thomas Darby** (h147) and **Itchy Feet** (h144), who finished second and third, respectively, in the Supreme. **City Island** (h151) and **Minella Indo** (h147) were the other big winners in this division at the Festival. The former failed to back up his Ballymore win at Punchestown, but there is no doubting the strength of his form, with the Cheltenham runner-up **Champ** (h149p) reinforcing what a good effort that was when winning the Sefton Novices' Hurdle at Aintree (by three lengths from **Emitom** (h146p)). Minella Indo, on the other hand, had no trouble following up his Albert Bartlett success at Punchestown, again looking better the further he went, and he appeals as the type to take high rank amongst this season's staying novice chasers. Cheltenham came too soon for **Reserve Tank** (h150p), but he showed himself to be an exciting prospect with Grade 1 wins at both Aintree and Punchestown, holding on in determined fashion on the latter occasion to beat **Sams Profile** (h150) by half a length. **Commander of Fleet** (h145) and **Quick Grabim** (h145) also won Grade 1s in Ireland during the latest campaign, while **Al Dancer** (h144) and **Getaway Trump** (h153p) both posted big efforts in winning handicaps, the latter looking particularly exciting when landing a valuable heat on the final day of the season at Sandown. As for the juvenile hurdlers, it was two horses trained by Nicky Henderson who ruled the roost following the demise of Triumph Hurdle favourite **Sir Erec** (h145), with **Fusil Raffles** (h147p) and **Pentland Hills** (h146p) cleaning up at the major spring festivals despite both only making their debuts for the yard in February.

2018/19 STATISTICS

TRAINERS (1,2,3 earnings)	Horses	Indiv'l Wnrs	Races Won	Runs	% Strike Rate	Stakes £
1 Paul Nicholls	161	76	135	589	22.9	3,158,852
2 Nicky Henderson	174	89	141	544	25.9	2,836,312
3 Dan Skelton	244	118	205	988	20.7	2,216,846
4 Colin Tizzard	129	51	77	600	12.8	1,753,171
5 W. P. Mullins, Ireland	63	8	8	74	10.8	1,336,423
6 Gordon Elliott, Ireland	120	35	55	206	26.7	1,309,852
7 Philip Hobbs	143	66	106	560	18.9	1,246,651
8 Alan King	139	57	91	499	18.2	1,202,795
9 Nigel Twiston-Davies	128	43	63	529	11.9	1,134,609
10 Tom George	103	38	52	377	13.8	803,454

JOCKEYS (by winners)	1st	2nd	3rd	Unpl	Total Rides	% Strike Rate
1 Richard Johnson	200	152	134	493	980	20.5
2 Harry Skelton	178	122	102	343	745	23.9
3 Brian Hughes	146	143	128	471	888	16.4
4 Harry Cobden	109	93	55	261	518	21.0
5 Sam Twiston-Davies	105	86	78	412	681	15.4
6 Aidan Coleman	95	68	90	329	582	16.3
7 Sean Bowen	91	79	65	360	595	15.3
8 Wayne Hutchinson	88	64	48	213	413	21.3
9 Nico de Boinville	86	56	32	207	381	22.6
10 Tom Scudamore	82	83	75	445	685	12.0

SIRES OF WINNERS (1,2,3 earnings)	Races Won	Runs	% Strike Rate	Stakes £
1 Flemensfirth (by Alleged)	83	640	13.0	1,478,239
2 Midnight Legend (by Night Shift)	123	748	16.4	1,440,832
3 Oscar (by Sadler's Wells)	92	690	13.3	1,429,805
4 King's Theatre (by Sadler's Wells)	92	540	17.0	1,382,778
5 Beneficial (by Top Ville)	93	685	13.6	1,159,298
6 Milan (by Sadler's Wells)	86	754	11.4	1,139,814
7 Westerner (by Danehill)	90	638	14.1	1,046,231
8 Kayf Tara (by Sadler's Wells)	68	758	9.0	1,042,281
9 Presenting (by Mtoto)	91	770	11.8	970,521
10 Stowaway (by Slip Anchor)	94	599	15.7	909,941

LEADING HORSES (1,2,3 earnings)	Races Won	Runs	Stakes £
1 Altior 9 b.g High Chaparral–Monte Solaro	5	5	562,145
2 Tiger Roll 9 b.g Authorized–Swiss Roll	2	3	540,235
3 Frodon 7 b.g Nickname–Miss Country	4	5	408,516
4 Al Boum Photo 7 b.g Buck's Boum–Al Gane	1	1	351,688
5 Paisley Park 7 b.g Oscar–Presenting Shares	5	5	347,744
6 Magic of Light 8 b.m Flemensfirth–Quest of Passion	2	5	261,939
7 Espoir d'Allen 5 b.g Voix du Nord–Quadanse	1	1	254,745
8 Clan des Obeaux 7 b.g Kapgarde–Nausicaa des Obeaux	2	5	215,080
9 If The Cap Fits 7 b.g Milan–Derravaragh Sayra	2	5	201,812
10 Silver Streak 6 gr.g Dark Angel–Happy Talk	2	7	199,755

SECTION

5

THE TIMEFORM TOP 100

Hurdlers

Rating	Horse
170	Espoir d'Allen
166p	Paisley Park
163	Buveur d'Air
162	Apple's Jade (f)
160+	Presenting Percy
159+	If The Cap Fits
159	Benie des Dieux (f)
159	Samcro
159	Verdana Blue (f)
158	Master Dino
158	Sam Spinner
157p	Klassical Dream
157+	Sharjah
157	Supasundae
156	Bapaume
156	Bedrock
156	Mr Adjudicator
156§	Wicklow Brave
155	Ch'tibello
155	Darasso
155	Petit Mouchoir
155	We Have A Dream
155x	Melon
154	Aux Ptits Soins
154	Call Me Lord
154	Faugheen
154	Laurina (f)
154	Midnight Shadow
154	Silver Streak
154	Tiger Roll
154	William Henry
153p	Getaway Trump
153	Global Citizen
153	Wholestone
153	Younevercall
152	Early Doors
152	Jezki
152	Summerville Boy
151+	Saldier
151	City Island
151	Off You Go
151	Sire du Berlais
151	Unowhatimeanharry
150p	Reserve Tank
150	Ballyandy
150	Old Guard
150	Sams Profile
150	Shaneshill
150§	West Approach
149p	Champ
149	Black Op
149	Brain Power
149	Roksana (f)
148	Minella Awards
148	Vision des Flos
147p	Fusil Raffles
147	Agrapart
147	Bacardys
147	Ballymoy
147	Killultagh Vic
147	Le Prezien
147	Lil Rockerfeller
147	Minella Indo
147	Mohaayed
147	Not Many Left
147	On The Blind Side
147	Thomas Darby
147	Tobefair
147	Tombstone
146p	Bright Forecast
146p	Emitom
146p	Pentland Hills
146	A Toi Phil
146	Bleu Berry
146	Brio Conti
146	Cracking Smart
146	Felix Desjy
146	Nautical Nitwit
146	Scarpeta
146	Shades of Midnight
146	Yorkhill
146§	Rashaan
145	Aramon
145	Commander of Fleet
145	Dallas des Pictons
145	Ivanovich Gorbatov
145	Pic d'Orhy
145	Quick Grabim
145	Saglawy
145	Stratum
145	Voix du Reve
144	Al Dancer
144	Asthuria (f)
144	Bachasson
144	Brewin'upastorm
144	Davids Charm
144	Grand Sancy
144	Itchy Feet
144	Ronald Pump
143p	Mister Fisher
143	De Name Escapes Me
143	Keeper Hill
143	Le Patriote
143	Thomas Campbell
143	Walk To Freedom

Chasers

Rating	Horse
180p	Altior
176	Kemboy
174	Al Boum Photo
174	Min
173+	Cyrname
170	Un de Sceaux
169p	Chacun Pour Soi
169x	Bristol de Mai
167	Anibale Fly
167	Frodon
167	Tiger Roll
166	Aso
166	Clan des Obeaux
166	Politologue
165+	Native River
165+	Presenting Percy
165	Bellshill
165	Monalee
165	Road To Respect
164p	Defi du Seuil
164	Balko des Flos
164	Fox Norton
164	Sceau Royal
164	Thistlecrack
163p	Delta Work
163	Definitly Red
162p	Topofthegame
162+	Duc des Genievres
162	Rathvinden
162	Simply Ned
162	Top Notch
161p	Santini
161	Alpha des Obeaux
161	Elegant Escape
161	Footpad
161	Janika
160p	Lostintranslation
160	Ballyoisin
160	Black Corton
160	The Storyteller
160§	Outlander
159p	Real Steel
159	God's Own
159	Invitation Only
158p	Le Richebourg
158	Hell's Kitchen
158	Terrefort
157	A Plus Tard
157	Cadmium
157	Charbel
157	Coneygree
157	Hammersly Lake
157	Lake View Lad
157	Sizing Tennessee
157§	Beware The Bear
156+	Voix du Reve
156	Castlegrace Paddy
156	Cloudy Dream
156	Great Field
156	Jury Duty
156	Saint Calvados
156	Shattered Love (f)
156	Snow Falcon
156	Sub Lieutenant
155	Acapella Bourgeois
155	Coney Island
155	Double Shuffle
155	Gold Present
155	Kildisart
155	Magic of Light (f)
155	Ordinary World
155	Ozzie The Oscar
155	Pairofbrowneyes
155	Sizing Codelco

155	Talkischeap
155	Valtor
155	Virgilio
155	Yala Enki
154p	Burrows Saint
154p	Cilaos Emery
154p	Kalashnikov
154p	Tout Est Permis
154	A Toi Phil
154	Dolos
154	Edwulf
154	Go Conquer
154	O O Seven
154	Waiting Patiently
153p	Kaiser Black
153+	Dynamite Dollars
153	Baron Alco
153	Clarcam
153	Forest Bihan
153	Hardline
153	Mister Whitaker
153	San Benedeto
153	Total Recall
152	Dounikos
152	Isleofhopendreams
152	Otago Trail
152	Ramses de Teillee
152	Robinsfirth

Juvenile Hurdlers

147p	Fusil Raffles
146p	Pentland Hills
145	Pic d'Orhy
143	Fakir d'Oudairies
143	Sir Erec
142p	Gardens of Babylon
142	French Made (f)
141	Coeur Sublime
139	Band of Outlaws
138	Chief Justice
135	Quel Destin
134	Cracker Factory
134	Tiger Tap Tap
133	Christopher Wood
132	Nelson River
132	Rocky Blue
131	Coko Beach
131	Way Back Home
130	Adjali

130	Havingagoodtime (f)
129p	Ecco
129p	Lucky Lover Boy
129	Fanfan du Seuil
129	Surin (f)
128	Chica Buena (f)
128	Naturelle (f)
127p	Morosini
127p	Vision du Puy (f)
127	Got Trumped
127	Torpillo

Novice Hurdlers

157p	Klassical Dream
153p	Getaway Trump
151	City Island
150p	Reserve Tank
150	Sams Profile
149p	Champ
147	Minella Indo
147	Thomas Darby
146p	Bright Forecast
146p	Emitom
146	Felix Desjy
145	Aramon
145	Commander of Fleet
145	Dallas des Pictons
145	Quick Grabim
144	Al Dancer
144	Brewin'upastorm
144	Grand Sancy
144	Itchy Feet
144	Ronald Pump
143p	Mister Fisher
142p	Battleoverdoyen
142	Canardier
142	Rouge Vif
141p	Tornado Flyer
141	Dorrells Pierji
141	Eglantine du Seuil (f)
141	Elixir de Nutz
141	Rhinestone
141	Triplicate

Novice Chasers

169p	Chacun Pour Soi
164p	Defi du Seuil
163p	Delta Work

162p	Topofthegame
162+	Duc des Genievres
161p	Santini
160p	Lostintranslation
159p	Real Steel
158p	Le Richebourg
157	A Plus Tard
156+	Voix du Reve
155	Kildisart
155	Talkischeap
154p	Burrows Saint
154p	Cilaos Emery
154p	Kalashnikov
153p	Kaiser Black
153+	Dynamite Dollars
153	Hardline
151p	La Bague Au Roi (f)
151	Ballyward
151	Mengli Khan
151	Ornua
150p	Master Dino
150	Getabird
150	Glen Forsa
150	Spiritofthegames
150	Top Ville Ben
150	Us And Them
149§	Duca de Thaix

NH Flat Horses

125	Envoi Allen
121+	Blue Sari
121	Thyme Hill
119	Get In The Queue
118	Abacadabras
117	Gypsy Island (f)
117p	Beacon Edge
117p	Malone Road
116p	King Roland
116	Embittered
116	Mcfabulous
115p	Festival d'Ex
113	Colreevy (f)
113	Sempo
112	Eden du Houx
112	Stick With Bill
111p	Thatsy
111	December Second
110p	Longhouse Poet
110	Imperial Alcazar

110	Meticulous
110	The Glancing Queen (f)
109	Daylight Katie (f)
109	Enrilo
109	Flic Ou Voyou
109	Master Debonair
109	Midnight Run
109	Nobby
108+	Enemy Coast Ahead
108	Montego Grey
108	Santa Rossa (f)

Hunter Chasers

137	Hazel Hill
136+	Caid Du Berlais
135	Burning Ambition
134	Road To Rome
134	Top Wood
133+	Shantou Flyer
133	Risk A Fine
132	Sizing Rome
131	Monsieur Gibraltar
131$	Wonderful Charm
130	Mr Mercurial
130	Virak
129	Bishops Road
129	Fennos Storm
129	Ucello Conti
128	Seefood
128	Stand Up And Fight
128	The Last But One
127	Mendip Express
127	Sizing Coal

* Indicates best performance achieved in a race other than a hunter chase

PROMISING HORSES

A p symbol is used by Timeform to denote horses we believe are capable of improvement, with a P symbol suggesting a horse is capable of much better form. Below is a list of selected British and Irish-trained horses with a p or P, listed under their current trainers.

KIM BAILEY
Alfie Corbitt (IRE) 6 b.g ... h95p
Espoir de Romay (FR) 5b.g ... h95p
Illuminated Beauty (IRE) 6 b.g ... h104p
Imperial Aura (IRE) 6 b.g ... h123p
Mr Macho (IRE) 7 b.g ... h116p
Pond Road (FR) 5 ch.g ... h83p b85
Robin The Raven (IRE) 7 b.g ... h138 c134p
Two For Gold (IRE) 6 b.g ... h132p
Vinndication (IRE) 6 b.g ... c148p

PETER BOWEN
Bang Bang Rosie (IRE) 7 b.m ... h115 c106p
Fortunes Hiding (IRE) 6 b.g ... h100p b99
No Quarter Asked (IRE) 4 b.g ... b89p
Rooster Cogburn (IRE) 6 b.g ... h101p

HENRY DE BROMHEAD, IRELAND
Honeysuckle 5 b.m ... h140p
Insult (IRE) 6 b.g ... h130p
Walk Away (IRE) 6 b.g ... h132p

MICK CHANNON
Glen Forsa (IRE) 7 b.g ... h119p c150
Hats Off To Larry 5 b.g ... h106p
Heydour (IRE) 6 br.g ... h107 c126p
Hold The Note (IRE) 5 b.g ... h126p b105

STUART EDMUNDS
Clondaw Native (IRE) 7 b.g ... h118 c89p
Deputy's Oscar (IRE) 6 b.g ... h79p b75
Maria's Benefit (IRE) 7 b.m ... c138p
Queenohearts (IRE) 6 ch.m ... h130p
Theclocksticking (IRE) 7 br.g ... h133 c132p

GORDON ELLIOTT, IRELAND
Andy Dufresne (IRE) 5 b.g ... b106P
Barra (FR) 8 b.m ... c130p
Battleoverdoyen (IRE) 6 b.g ... h142p b107
Braid Blue (IRE) 6 b.g ... h120p b101
Champagne Classic (IRE) 8 b.g ... c145p
Chosen Mate (IRE) 6 b.g ... h137p
Delta Work (FR) 6 br.g ... c163p
Festival d'Ex (FR) 4 b.g ... b115p
Glenloe (IRE) 8 br.g ... c130p
Its All Guesswork (IRE) 7 b.g ... h121 c125p
Make My Heart Fly (IRE) 7 b.m ... h124 c112p
Malone Road (IRE) 5 b.g ... b117p
Markhan (USA) 6 b.g ... h115p
Thatsy (FR) 5 gr.g ... b111p

PETER FAHEY, IRELAND
Gypsy Island (IRE) 5 b.m ... h105P b117

HARRY FRY
Any Drama (IRE) 8 b.g ... c115p
Dalila du Seuil (FR) 6 gr.m ... c132p
Deadringerforlove 5 b.m ... h102p b88

Ena Baie (FR) 5 b.m ... h102p
Gameface (IRE) 5 b.g ... h65p
Ishkhara Lady 5 b.m ... b104p
King Roland (IRE) 5 br.g ... b116p
Phoenix Way (IRE) 6 b.g ... h119p

NICK GIFFORD
Glen Rocco 8 ch.g ... c135p

CHRIS GORDON
Baddesley Prince (IRE) 5 b.g ... h116p
Shut The Box (IRE) 5 ch.g ... h106p b86

WARREN GREATREX
Emitom (IRE) 5 b.g ... h146p b96
La Bague Au Roi (FR) 8 b.m ... c151p
Portrush Ted (IRE) 7 b.g ... h119p

MRS J. HARRINGTON, IRELAND
Alletrix (IRE) 6 b.m ... h131 c111p
Morosini (FR) 4 b.g ... h127p

NICKY HENDERSON
Allart (IRE) 5 b.g ... b95p
Barbados Blue (IRE) 5 b.m ... h115p b94
Beyondthestorm (IRE) 6 b.g ... h86p
Champ (IRE) 7 b.g ... h149p
Champagne Mystery (IRE) 5 b.g ... h125p
Champagne Platinum (IRE) 5 gr.g ... h121p
Chantry House (IRE) 5 b.g ... b104p
Claimantakinforgan (FR) 7 b.g ... c139p
Daphne du Clos (FR) 6 b.m ... h100P
El Kaldoun (FR) 5 b.g ... h99p b93
Epatante (FR) 5 b.m ... h123p
Floressa (FR) 4 b.f ... b97p
Fusil Raffles (FR) 4 b.g ... h147p
Humphrey Bogart (IRE) 6 b.g ... h116p
Italian Summer 4 br.f ... b77p
Jen's Boy 5 b.g ... h89p b85
Lisheen Castle (IRE) 4 b.g ... h108p
Loveherandleaveher (IRE) 7 b. or br.m ... h108p
Mister Fisher (IRE) 5 b.g ... h143p
Never Adapt (FR) 4 ch.f ... h118p
Ok Corral (IRE) 9 b.g ... c148p
Pacific de Baune (FR) 6 gr.g ... h122 c131p
Pentland Hills (IRE) 4 b.g ... h146p
Pistol Whipped (IRE) 5 b.g ... h124p
Precious Cargo (IRE) 6 b.g ... h126p
Rathhill (IRE) 6 b.g ... h125p
Santini 7 b.g ... c161p
Shishkin (IRE) 5 b.g ... b104p
Storm of Intrigue (IRE) 7 b.g ... h114p
Style de Vole (FR) 4 gr.g ... h120p
Sunrise Ruby 5 ch.m ... h116p b97
Sunshade 6 b.m ... h137p
Trull La La 5 ch.m ... h108p

PHILIP HOBBS
Defi du Seuil (FR) 6 b.g ... c164p
Deise Aba (IRE) 6 b.g ... h121p
Earth Moor (IRE) 5 ch.g ... h107p b97
Evidence de Thaix (FR) 5 b.m ... h109p
Flinck (IRE) 5 b.g ... h106p
I'm A Game Changer (IRE) 7 b.g ... h137 c127p
Mcnamaras Band (IRE) 6 b.g ... h120p
Musical Slave (IRE) 5 b.g ... h128p
Ninth Wave (IRE) 5 b.g ... h99 c87p b89
No Comment 8 br.g ... c131p
Oakley (IRE) 6 b.g ... h131p
Pileon (IRE) 5 b.g ... b99p
Smarty Wild 5 b.g ... h129p b70
Westend Story (IRE) 8 b.g ... c137p

ANTHONY HONEYBALL
Deja Vue (IRE) 5 b.g ... h80p
Hideaway Vic (IRE) 6 b.g ... h111p
Marilyn Monroe (IRE) 6 b.m ... b89p
Shapiro 6 b.m ... h108p
Sojourn (IRE) 6 b.g ... h110p b100

ALAN KING
Smith's Bay 6 b.g ... h106p
Timoteo (FR) 6 b.g ... h106 c134p
Whenhellbrokeloose 6 b.g ... b68p

TOM LACEY
Capac (IRE) 4 ch.g ... b98p
Glory And Fortune (IRE) 4 b.g ... b99p
Hazzaar (IRE) 5 b.g ... b102p
L'Incorrigible (FR) 4 b.g ... b102p
Sebastopol (IRE) 5 b.g ... h113p
Sir Egbert 6 b.g ... c128p

EMMA LAVELLE
De Rasher Counter 7 b.g ... c145p
Fontsanta (IRE) 6 b.g ... h124p
Freedom Run 6 ch.m ... h84p b82
Highly Prized 6 b. or br.g ... h110p
Paisley Park (IRE) 7 b.g ... h166p
Silent Assistant (IRE) 5 b.g ... h109p

DONALD MCCAIN
Carry On 4 b.g ... b88p
First Account 5 b. or br.g ... h121p
Lord Springfield (IRE) 6 ch.g ... h103p
The Con Man (IRE) 5 b.g ... h119p
The Some Dance Kid (IRE) 6 b.g ... h122p

NOEL MEADE, IRELAND
Beacon Edge (IRE) 5 b.g ... b117p
Brace Yourself (IRE) 6 ch.g ... h115p
Tout Est Permis (FR) 6 gr.g ... c154p
Young Ted (IRE) 5 b.g ... h132p

GARY MOORE

Bullfrog (IRE) 6 b.m. h109p
Early du Lemo (FR) 6 gr.g. c136p
Episode (FR) 5 ch.m. h95p
Espion de Saflo (FR) 5 b.g. h117p
High Up In The Air (FR) 5 ch.g. h77p
Il Re di Nessuno (FR) 4 b.g. h92p

NEIL MULHOLLAND

Ballymilan 4 b.f. b79p
Dead Right 7 b.g. h120p
Deputy Jones (IRE) 6 b.m. h105p
Dramatic Approach 5 b.m. b86p
Global Rhapsody (IRE) 5 b.g. h80p
Golden Emblem (IRE) 5 ch.m. b88p
Vis A Vis 5 b.g. h117p

W. P. MULLINS, IRELAND

Bargy Lady (IRE) 7 b.m. h133 c128p
Breaken (FR) 5 b.g. h134p
Burrows Saint (FR) 6 b.g. c154p
Carefully Selected (IRE) 7 b.g. h137p
Chacun Pour Soi (FR) 7 b.g. c169p
Ciel de Neige (FR) 4 b.g. h126p
Cilaos Emery (FR) 7 b.g. c154p
Concertista 5 ch.m. h136p
Elfile (FR) 5 b.m. h135p
Klassical Dream (FR) 5 b.g. h157p
Ontheropes (IRE) 5 b.g. h130p b92
Real Steel (FR) 6 b.g. c159p
Relegate (IRE) 6 b.m. h125p
Royal Rendezvous (IRE) 7 b.g. h129p b113
Shanning 6 b.m. h136p
Timi Roli (FR) 7 b.g. h123 c133p
Tornado Flyer (IRE) 6 b.g. h141p

OLLY MURPHY

Adjutant 4 b.g. h105p
Blazer's Mill 5 b.g. b95p
Bon Calvados (FR) 5 b.g. b65p
Collooney (IRE) 5 b.g. h122p b100
Craigmor (IRE) 7 b.g. h101 c112p
Elena Sue 6 b.m. b79p
Emerald Rocket (IRE) 4 b.g. h115p
Georgiator (FR) 6 b.g. b91p
Monbeg Zena (IRE) 7 ch.m. h113p
Nickolson (FR) 5 b.g. b92p
Notre Pari (IRE) 5 b.g. h110p
Peachey (IRE) 5 b.g. h113p b86
Smart Getaway (IRE) 7 b.m. h98p b76
Time For Another (IRE) 6 b.g. h79p

DR RICHARD NEWLAND

Dashing Perk 8 b.g. c126p
Rose Sea Has (FR) 4 gr.g. h113 c123p

PAUL NICHOLLS

Accomplice (FR) 5 gr.g. h111p
Archie Brown (FR) 5 b.g. b88p
Casko d'Airy (FR) 7 b.g. h120p
Danny Kirwan (IRE) 6 b.g. h133p
Danny Whizzbang (IRE) 6 b.g. h128p
Dogon 4 b.g. h124 c127p
Ecco 4 b.g. h129p
Getaway Trump (IRE) 6 b.g. h153p
Greaneteen (FR) 5 b.g. h127p
Grey Getaway (IRE) 5 gr.g. b65p
Highland Hunter (IRE) 6 gr.g. h126p
Kapcorse (FR) 6 br.g. h103 c143p

Scaramanga (IRE) 4 b.g. h123p
Secret Investor 7 b.g. .... h134+ c147p
Topofthegame (IRE) 7 ch.g. c162p

FERGAL O'BRIEN

Phoenician Star (IRE) 4 ch.g. h118p
Pride of Lecale 8 b.g. h106p
Tequila Blaze 5 b.m. b72p

JOSEPH PATRICK O'BRIEN, IRELAND

Darasso (FR) 6 b.g. h155 c150p
Fakir d'Oudairies (FR) 4 b.g. h143 c96P
Gardens of Babylon (IRE) 4 b.g. h142p
Le Richebourg (FR) 6 br.g. h130 c158p
Monarch (IRE) 6 b.g. h138 c129p

JONJO O'NEILL

Cloth Cap (IRE) 7 b.g. c134p
Cobolobo (FR) 7 br.g. c129p
Flight Deck (IRE) 5 b.g. h96p
Generation Gap (IRE) 5 b.g. h100p
Notawordofalie (IRE) 4 br.f. b63p
Pagero (FR) 4 b.g. h112p
Palmers Hill (IRE) 6 b.g. h131p
Seaton Carew (IRE) 5 b.m. b91p
Sermando (FR) 5 ch.g. h106p
Tedham 5 b.g. h130p
The Crafty Touch (IRE) 6 ch.m. h90p

BEN PAULING

Bright Forecast (IRE) 5 b.g. h146p
Chess Player (IRE) 4 ch.g. b98p
The Captains Inn (IRE) 5 b.g. h125p b85
Towards The Dawn 5 b.g. h111p

DAVID PIPE

Delirant (FR) 6 b.g. h101p
First Lord de Cuet (FR) 5 gr.g. b100p
Jasmin des Bordes (FR) 5 b.g. h114p b94
Moon Racer (IRE) 10 b.g. h133 c124p
New Age Dawning (IRE) 5 ch.g. h119p b96
Yaa Salaam (IRE) 5 ch.g. h111p

NICKY RICHARDS

Elios d'Or (FR) 5 b.g. b85p
Glittering Love (IRE) 7 b.g. c125p
No Regrets (IRE) 5 b.g. b94p
Reivers Lad 8 b.g. c133p
Uncle Alastair 7 b.g. c142p

OLIVER SHERWOOD

Brummie Boys (IRE) 4 b.g. b80p
Cilaos Glace (FR) 6 br.g. c123p
Sammy Bill 6 b.g. h97p
Tarada 6 br.g. h123p b94

DAN SKELTON

Aggy With It (IRE) 5 b.m. b92p
Amoola Gold (GER) 6 b.g. h111 c125p
Annie Angel (IRE) 8 b.m. c91p
Anytime Will Do (IRE) 6 b.g. h131p
Bennys King (IRE) 8 b.g. c141p
Betameche (FR) 8 b.g. h126p
Beyondapproach (IRE) 5 b.m. h91p
Blairs Cove 7 b.g. c108p
Bourbon Borderline (IRE) 5 b.g. b96p
Floki (IRE) 5 b.g. h87p b83
Humble Hero (IRE) 5 b.g. h129p
I'd Better Go Now (IRE) 6 b.g. h84p
Interconnected 5 br.g. h122p

Jane Lamb 6 b.m. h98p
Magellan 5 b.g. h101p
Marada 4 ch.f. b81p
Molly The Dolly (IRE) 8 b.m. c144p
No Getaway (IRE) 6 ch.g. h114p
Northofthewall (IRE) 5 b.g. h103p b76
Percy's Word 5 b.g. h110p
Protektorat (FR) 4 b.g. h122p
Sense of Adventure (IRE) 5 ch.g. b85p
Shan Blue (IRE) 5 b.g. b98p
Sofia's Rock (FR) 5 b.g. h137p
Tigeralley 10 b.m. h105 c91p
Vision du Puy (FR) 4 b.f. h127p

COLIN TIZZARD

Copperhead 5 ch.g. h121p
Eldorado Allen (FR) 5 gr.g. h115p
Faustinovick 5 b.g. b93p
Jaytrack Parkhomes 5 b.g. h80p b98
L'Air du Vent (FR) 5 b.g. b101P
Lostintranslation (IRE) 7 b.g. c160p
Pingshou (IRE) 9 b.g. c120p
Reserve Tank (IRE) 5 b.g. h150p

NIGEL TWISTON-DAVIES

Blue Flight (FR) 5 b.g. c147p
Florrie Boy (IRE) 8 b.g. h117 c123p
Guy (IRE) 4 b.g. b93p
Milanstorm (IRE) 6 b.g. h92p

EVAN WILLIAMS

Annsam 4 b.g. h91p
Esprit du Large (FR) 5 b.g. h120p b72
Keeping Faith (IRE) 5 br.m. h92p
Mac Amara 5 b.m. h94p b96
Mouseinthehouse (IRE) 5 b.g. h90p
No Rematch (IRE) 5 b.g. h112p b84
The Last Day (IRE) 7 b.g. c132p

IAN WILLIAMS

Cracking Destiny (IRE) 6 b.g. h95p c113
Monjeni 6 b.g. h81p
Paddy The Chef (IRE) 4 b.g. h106p
Psychedelic Rock 8 b.g. h129 c133p
Speedo Boy 5 ch.g. h121p
The Grand Visir 5 b.g. h99p
Yellow Dockets (IRE) 7 ch.m. h121p b75

NICK WILLIAMS

Favori de Sivola (FR) 4 b.g. h95p
Le Grand Rocher (FR) 3 b.g. h110p
One For The Team 5 b.g. h109p
Prudhomme (FR) 4 ch.g. b100p
Siruh du Lac (FR) 6 b.g. c147p

VENETIA WILLIAMS

Commodore (FR) 7 gr.g. c126p
Destinee Royale (FR) 6 b.m. h101p
Geordie B 6 gr.g. h124p
Longhousesignora (IRE) 7 b.m. h110 c101p
Yalltari 8 gr.g. c140p

TRAINERS FOR COURSES

The following statistics show the most successful trainers over the past five seasons at each of the courses that stage National Hunt racing in England, Scotland and Wales. Impact Value is expressed as a factor of a trainer's number of winners compared to those expected to occur by chance. Market Value is expressed as the factor by which the % chance of an Industry Starting Price exceeds random, as implied by field size. For example, a horse that is shorter than 3/1 in a 4-runner field will have a Market Value above 1.

AINTREE

Trainer	Wins	Runs	Strike Rate	% Rivals Beaten	P/L	Run To Form %	Impact Value	Market Value
Nicky Henderson	28	143	19.58%	59.52	8.11	24.93	1.97	1.81
Paul Nicholls	17	148	11.49%	54.10	-49.63	15.01	1.24	1.71
Dan Skelton	15	111	13.51%	60.16	-1.95	26.71	1.22	1.41
Colin Tizzard	14	62	22.58%	62.13	111.49	33.87	2.52	1.42
W. P. Mullins, Ireland	11	63	17.46%	58.69	-8.15	30.16	2.12	2.15
Tom George	10	82	12.20%	52.76	-0.67	22.37	1.35	1.35
Nigel Twiston-Davies	10	105	9.52%	52.33	-49.75	16.57	1.05	1.53
Philip Hobbs	8	84	9.52%	49.49	-39.30	13.33	1.16	1.52
Gordon Elliott, Ireland	8	64	12.50%	58.19	-9.00	21.87	1.99	1.87
Jonjo O'Neill	8	87	9.20%	45.77	-34.21	14.16	0.98	1.46

ASCOT

Trainer	Wins	Runs	Strike Rate	% Rivals Beaten	P/L	Run To Form %	Impact Value	Market Value
Paul Nicholls	35	179	19.55%	57.11	22.42	31.08	1.47	1.54
Nicky Henderson	33	158	20.89%	62.27	-6.25	33.30	1.70	1.87
Harry Fry	17	63	26.98%	63.85	10.34	36.98	2.39	1.82
Alan King	11	87	12.64%	57.03	-38.71	25.46	1.18	1.55
Philip Hobbs	10	90	11.11%	57.42	-14.59	24.89	0.91	1.34
Venetia Williams	10	76	13.16%	48.87	12.75	21.05	1.11	1.10
David Pipe	9	49	18.37%	57.36	11.75	26.53	1.72	1.05
Gary Moore	8	92	8.70%	41.74	-33.50	15.63	0.72	0.87
Colin Tizzard	7	72	9.72%	50.32	-37.22	32.58	0.74	0.99
Charlie Longsdon	6	51	11.76%	42.25	21.00	13.96	1.07	1.04

AYR

Trainer	Wins	Runs	Strike Rate	% Rivals Beaten	P/L	Run To Form %	Impact Value	Market Value
Nicky Richards	43	185	23.24%	59.95	-3.05	36.84	1.85	2.02
Lucinda Russell	32	299	10.70%	51.49	-135.37	24.14	0.81	1.06
N. W. Alexander	28	247	11.34%	49.56	-58.23	22.12	0.92	0.93
Donald McCain	15	91	16.48%	47.11	-35.74	23.78	1.16	1.38
Dan Skelton	15	54	27.78%	67.01	5.07	40.74	2.23	1.88
Stuart Crawford, Ireland	14	129	10.85%	51.38	-57.98	24.47	0.87	1.24
James Ewart	13	107	12.15%	54.81	-25.45	22.61	1.01	1.10
Iain Jardine	13	72	18.06%	54.16	2.48	25.69	1.48	1.14
Sandy Thomson	11	68	16.18%	59.75	-22.65	33.78	1.47	1.50
Martin Todhunter	11	69	15.94%	53.09	11.23	23.58	1.26	1.09

BANGOR-ON-DEE

Trainer	Wins	Runs	Strike Rate	% Rivals Beaten	P/L	Run To Form %	Impact Value	Market Value
Donald McCain	63	324	19.44%	56.99	22.80	30.26	1.36	1.29
Dan Skelton	27	106	25.47%	61.41	-6.82	39.88	2.07	1.96
Alan King	19	67	28.36%	66.58	-8.75	40.75	2.01	2.19
Jonjo O'Neill	14	105	13.33%	48.73	-20.13	18.82	1.07	1.24
Henry Daly	14	56	25.00%	59.91	50.75	41.21	2.15	1.25
Warren Greatrex	12	50	24.00%	59.58	-10.36	30.59	1.82	2.01
Charlie Longsdon	11	63	17.46%	51.65	-8.03	25.40	1.19	1.36
Kim Bailey	11	55	20.00%	52.14	-22.18	25.78	1.65	1.76
Nigel Twiston-Davies	11	69	15.94%	57.97	-18.36	29.31	1.26	1.55
Rebecca Curtis	10	55	18.18%	55.40	-8.67	32.76	1.23	1.47

CARLISLE

Trainer	Wins	Runs	Strike Rate	% Rivals Beaten	P/L	Run To Form %	Impact Value	Market Value
Donald McCain	27	205	13.17%	56.76	-53.14	22.40	0.96	1.37
Sue Smith	20	125	16.00%	51.49	-21.59	22.57	1.23	1.24
Nicky Richards	19	86	22.09%	55.49	30.94	29.28	1.69	1.47
Stuart Crawford, Ireland	14	37	37.84%	70.76	12.14	44.73	2.96	2.00
Micky Hammond	13	128	10.16%	42.75	-34.85	15.87	0.75	0.85
Venetia Williams	11	42	26.19%	51.34	15.03	37.04	1.98	1.79
Brian Ellison	10	60	16.67%	57.93	-28.79	28.41	1.39	1.74
Jennie Candlish	9	67	13.43%	52.61	-24.13	19.45	1.12	0.95
Nigel Hawke	9	27	33.33%	73.29	5.37	41.81	2.48	1.61
Nigel Twiston-Davies	9	25	36.00%	64.95	9.92	46.80	2.84	2.53

TRAINERS FOR COURSES

CARTMEL

Trainer	Wins	Runs	Strike Rate	% Rivals Beaten	P/L	Run To Form %	Impact Value	Market Value
Donald McCain	28	134	20.90%	61.18	-10.87	28.10	1.50	1.48
James Moffatt	23	218	10.55%	49.44	-36.88	16.37	0.84	1.04
Peter Bowen	21	64	32.81%	65.96	26.72	39.58	2.57	1.86
Gordon Elliott, Ireland	10	38	26.32%	70.25	-4.55	47.56	2.18	2.41
Micky Hammond	9	79	11.39%	50.53	-24.50	20.52	0.94	1.14
Martin Todhunter	8	55	14.55%	55.99	-15.63	25.90	1.19	1.34
Dianne Sayer	8	106	7.55%	44.35	-59.17	12.36	0.65	1.03
Jonjo O'Neill	7	26	26.92%	63.49	4.80	34.62	1.87	1.66
Julia Brooke	6	26	23.08%	62.17	11.33	31.82	2.31	1.20
Neil Mulholland	5	23	21.74%	47.80	-6.30	23.60	1.29	1.55

CATTERICK BRIDGE

Trainer	Wins	Runs	Strike Rate	% Rivals Beaten	P/L	Run To Form %	Impact Value	Market Value
Sue Smith	27	90	30.00%	64.39	58.83	39.63	2.32	1.48
Donald McCain	27	152	17.76%	58.84	-19.10	29.93	1.35	1.42
Brian Ellison	15	58	25.86%	64.30	-16.95	41.38	1.88	2.05
Micky Hammond	12	168	7.14%	46.80	-58.00	15.62	0.59	0.74
Dan Skelton	8	33	24.24%	56.12	-11.61	30.30	1.73	2.39
Rebecca Menzies	7	34	20.59%	64.27	-1.79	35.29	1.52	1.13
John Quinn	6	23	26.09%	68.57	-4.97	50.00	2.24	2.91
Sam England	5	25	20.00%	58.92	-0.75	42.25	1.37	1.18
Jamie Snowden	5	11	45.45%	78.64	1.33	63.64	2.90	1.77
Alan King	4	6	66.67%	88.61	1.74	83.33	4.87	3.84

CHELTENHAM

Trainer	Wins	Runs	Strike Rate	% Rivals Beaten	P/L	Run To Form %	Impact Value	Market Value
Nicky Henderson	44	378	11.64%	54.15	-109.86	23.70	1.30	1.68
Paul Nicholls	41	354	11.58%	53.66	11.84	23.21	1.20	1.49
W. P. Mullins, Ireland	33	300	11.00%	55.83	-18.73	28.78	1.62	1.83
Philip Hobbs	27	231	11.69%	54.97	-57.88	22.36	1.27	1.49
Nigel Twiston-Davies	27	263	10.27%	52.31	-89.40	23.38	1.08	1.23
Gordon Elliott, Ireland	26	187	13.90%	58.87	40.60	28.34	2.04	1.87
Colin Tizzard	24	244	9.84%	49.03	-86.02	22.03	1.01	1.11
Alan King	19	169	11.24%	52.43	-20.67	24.26	1.32	1.21
Dan Skelton	19	194	9.79%	54.52	-40.29	22.29	1.07	1.29
Fergal O'Brien	17	146	11.64%	56.06	17.63	30.99	1.39	1.11

CHEPSTOW

Trainer	Wins	Runs	Strike Rate	% Rivals Beaten	P/L	Run To Form %	Impact Value	Market Value
Paul Nicholls	35	154	22.73%	62.24	-17.74	34.81	2.01	2.16
Philip Hobbs	35	167	20.96%	58.53	-10.07	30.52	2.08	2.05
Evan Williams	34	204	16.67%	56.52	77.37	24.03	1.52	1.38
Colin Tizzard	20	189	10.58%	55.64	-68.13	26.46	0.99	1.38
Peter Bowen	19	122	15.57%	52.61	-10.47	25.15	1.45	1.13
Nigel Twiston-Davies	19	109	17.43%	60.25	3.27	24.51	1.70	1.55
Venetia Williams	18	130	13.85%	53.95	-37.32	26.51	1.27	1.31
David Pipe	18	113	15.93%	62.30	-20.55	26.46	1.57	1.64
Tom George	16	80	20.00%	53.35	-21.04	25.81	1.97	1.62
Jonjo O'Neill	14	120	11.67%	52.81	-42.99	22.59	1.19	1.36

DONCASTER

Trainer	Wins	Runs	Strike Rate	% Rivals Beaten	P/L	Run To Form %	Impact Value	Market Value
Nicky Henderson	26	78	33.33%	70.10	-1.46	56.79	2.44	2.69
Alan King	24	115	20.87%	59.54	-5.40	32.32	1.53	1.66
Paul Nicholls	18	70	25.71%	55.53	-13.95	36.29	1.60	1.78
Ben Pauling	13	52	25.00%	49.00	23.15	34.12	1.95	1.52
Emma Lavelle	12	45	26.67%	62.02	9.15	33.33	2.38	1.66
Dan Skelton	11	82	13.41%	53.46	-45.29	30.34	1.02	1.37
Ian Williams	11	74	14.86%	49.53	-1.83	25.42	1.17	1.05
Charlie Longsdon	11	90	12.22%	51.64	-18.80	33.25	1.01	1.21
Jonjo O'Neill	11	93	11.83%	52.66	-21.75	19.81	1.17	1.09
Kim Bailey	11	59	18.64%	53.81	-24.44	30.51	1.53	1.75

EXETER

Trainer	Wins	Runs	Strike Rate	% Rivals Beaten	P/L	Run To Form %	Impact Value	Market Value
Philip Hobbs	51	238	21.43%	61.09	-49.59	35.25	1.72	1.98
Paul Nicholls	44	141	31.21%	67.17	-7.69	44.47	2.20	2.65
Colin Tizzard	33	193	17.10%	59.48	-48.95	27.20	1.45	1.50
Harry Fry	29	79	36.71%	74.99	44.78	54.78	3.23	2.81
David Pipe	23	200	11.50%	52.62	-68.53	19.59	1.06	1.38
Evan Williams	17	76	22.37%	51.14	31.63	28.36	1.63	1.17
Alan King	16	87	18.39%	61.84	-21.11	37.30	1.62	1.87
Venetia Williams	13	89	14.61%	49.56	-8.47	25.06	1.23	1.32
Susan Gardner	13	130	10.00%	46.87	-51.38	17.15	0.90	0.86
Victor Dartnall	12	101	11.88%	55.62	-36.88	25.75	1.14	1.31

TRAINERS FOR COURSES

FAKENHAM

Trainer	Wins	Runs	Strike Rate	% Rivals Beaten	P/L	Run To Form %	Impact Value	Market Value
Olly Murphy	24	89	26.97%	62.64	13.14	40.36	1.55	1.50
Lucy Wadham	20	72	27.78%	60.40	18.10	36.81	1.88	1.49
Neil Mulholland	17	51	33.33%	60.20	12.76	41.18	2.15	1.56
Dan Skelton	16	72	22.22%	60.37	-17.42	29.17	1.32	1.70
Nicky Henderson	13	38	34.21%	62.97	-11.33	53.33	1.98	2.48
Neil King	12	83	14.46%	50.47	15.03	23.80	0.90	1.03
Stuart Edmunds	8	24	33.33%	67.29	30.67	48.04	2.06	1.28
Christian Williams	8	23	34.78%	64.20	3.19	55.00	2.19	1.63
Alex Hales	7	46	15.22%	55.66	-4.27	26.09	1.05	1.04
Charlie Mann	7	28	25.00%	45.56	14.00	33.39	1.58	1.11

FFOS LAS

Trainer	Wins	Runs	Strike Rate	% Rivals Beaten	P/L	Run To Form %	Impact Value	Market Value
Evan Williams	49	328	14.94%	53.37	-42.73	24.80	1.11	1.22
Peter Bowen	39	251	15.54%	55.80	-80.05	25.73	1.13	1.25
Nigel Twiston-Davies	33	157	21.02%	60.68	-11.91	31.63	1.58	1.55
Rebecca Curtis	29	121	23.97%	58.77	13.40	34.14	1.83	1.71
Warren Greatrex	13	51	25.49%	57.35	-6.83	37.91	1.87	2.17
Nicky Henderson	12	33	36.36%	65.93	-9.69	65.22	2.61	2.98
Debra Hamer	12	83	14.46%	47.22	-4.63	24.54	1.15	0.99
Bernard Llewellyn	12	88	13.64%	51.92	-5.98	17.73	0.95	0.90
Jonjo O'Neill	12	82	14.63%	54.14	-27.17	21.24	1.15	1.39
David Rees	11	105	10.48%	49.86	8.13	17.58	0.84	0.97

FONTWELL PARK

Trainer	Wins	Runs	Strike Rate	% Rivals Beaten	P/L	Run To Form %	Impact Value	Market Value
Gary Moore	58	360	16.11%	52.84	-42.43	27.07	1.15	1.34
Chris Gordon	40	263	15.21%	52.35	-26.32	22.00	1.13	1.19
Neil Mulholland	39	182	21.43%	58.01	-9.71	33.50	1.46	1.31
Paul Nicholls	37	91	40.66%	70.94	8.13	49.38	2.24	2.19
Colin Tizzard	28	132	21.21%	57.88	-19.52	32.07	1.52	1.51
Anthony Honeyball	27	83	32.53%	68.02	26.30	46.12	2.06	1.77
Dan Skelton	22	105	20.95%	60.44	-20.46	30.82	1.45	1.71
Alan King	19	64	29.69%	65.03	2.22	41.72	2.21	2.24
Seamus Mullins	19	163	11.66%	48.25	-15.92	21.23	0.88	0.96
Philip Hobbs	17	67	25.37%	63.95	-20.98	41.51	1.77	2.30

HAYDOCK PARK

Trainer	Wins	Runs	Strike Rate	% Rivals Beaten	P/L	Run To Form %	Impact Value	Market Value
Nigel Twiston-Davies	20	109	18.35%	57.43	-15.24	29.43	1.52	1.32
Paul Nicholls	16	70	22.86%	57.63	-18.45	29.22	1.59	1.73
Sue Smith	15	117	12.82%	59.16	-0.38	27.98	0.99	1.26
Donald McCain	14	99	14.14%	48.40	-33.97	19.35	1.03	0.95
Venetia Williams	13	73	17.81%	52.34	58.38	24.66	1.42	1.45
David Pipe	12	65	18.46%	57.58	44.00	21.54	1.87	1.35
Nicky Henderson	10	44	22.73%	57.80	-13.58	32.84	1.52	1.84
Tom George	9	43	20.93%	52.87	-2.17	24.71	1.84	1.61
Dan Skelton	7	77	9.09%	49.19	-40.13	16.88	0.71	1.30
Evan Williams	7	71	9.86%	49.70	-8.50	21.54	0.78	1.12

HEREFORD

Trainer	Wins	Runs	Strike Rate	% Rivals Beaten	P/L	Run To Form %	Impact Value	Market Value
Venetia Williams	11	56	19.64%	46.33	6.23	21.82	1.71	1.31
Warren Greatrex	7	24	29.17%	75.96	-2.37	54.63	2.52	2.45
Philip Hobbs	6	32	18.75%	65.50	-13.23	39.29	1.57	2.35
Dan Skelton	6	32	18.75%	54.55	-2.56	25.22	1.52	1.75
Evan Williams	6	56	10.71%	46.31	-33.10	16.22	0.84	1.26
Henry Oliver	6	36	16.67%	55.96	13.00	23.00	1.50	1.06
Alan King	5	15	33.33%	65.43	-0.48	40.00	3.08	2.76
Kerry Lee	5	44	11.36%	56.02	-21.55	18.36	0.91	1.30
Tom George	5	26	19.23%	62.18	-4.67	27.69	1.67	1.58
David Rees	4	13	30.77%	52.09	12.88	36.36	2.85	1.19

HEXHAM

Trainer	Wins	Runs	Strike Rate	% Rivals Beaten	P/L	Run To Form %	Impact Value	Market Value
Lucinda Russell	35	236	14.83%	55.30	3.06	24.11	1.23	1.35
Micky Hammond	21	180	11.67%	49.68	-60.74	19.32	1.06	1.18
Maurice Barnes	21	151	13.91%	53.78	-26.88	24.15	1.22	1.05
Nicky Richards	16	49	32.65%	61.43	15.38	39.70	2.91	2.10
Mark Walford	14	72	19.44%	62.92	5.78	31.92	1.74	1.55
Brian Ellison	13	66	19.70%	58.58	-3.18	30.45	1.60	1.69
Stuart Coltherd	12	82	14.63%	55.23	21.25	21.47	1.32	1.37
Donald McCain	11	99	11.11%	50.26	-69.56	17.28	0.82	1.69
George Bewley	11	78	14.10%	47.03	6.75	19.83	1.27	0.88
James Ewart	11	59	18.64%	55.46	0.25	24.71	1.73	1.36

TRAINERS FOR COURSES

HUNTINGDON

Trainer	Wins	Runs	Strike Rate	% Rivals Beaten	P/L	Run To Form %	Impact Value	Market Value
Nicky Henderson	31	105	29.52%	66.09	-21.26	42.37	2.31	2.51
Jonjo O'Neill	24	120	20.00%	53.62	4.13	27.17	1.68	1.47
Dan Skelton	24	153	15.69%	58.17	-55.38	30.05	1.24	1.71
Kim Bailey	23	108	21.30%	55.60	25.48	37.68	1.73	1.36
Alan King	23	112	20.54%	68.39	-31.68	41.42	1.62	2.35
Gary Moore	16	113	14.16%	50.97	8.83	26.55	1.13	1.24
Ben Pauling	14	75	18.67%	54.25	74.15	26.62	1.60	1.58
David Dennis	11	50	22.00%	59.02	22.46	30.00	1.84	1.15
Fergal O'Brien	10	45	22.22%	61.85	45.46	28.89	1.72	1.33
Charlie Longsdon	10	97	10.31%	45.67	-46.52	24.71	0.82	1.07

KELSO

Trainer	Wins	Runs	Strike Rate	% Rivals Beaten	P/L	Run To Form %	Impact Value	Market Value
Lucinda Russell	37	259	14.29%	54.27	-46.59	24.16	1.14	1.18
Nicky Richards	31	132	23.48%	59.93	14.03	30.69	1.72	1.83
Donald McCain	25	158	15.82%	54.75	-47.84	22.69	1.16	1.55
N. W. Alexander	25	189	13.23%	49.27	-6.86	20.43	1.09	0.98
James Ewart	15	94	15.96%	53.31	17.13	25.04	1.31	1.17
Sandy Thomson	15	112	13.39%	57.24	40.70	29.02	1.07	1.21
Rose Dobbin	13	129	10.08%	52.91	-63.06	17.15	0.89	1.21
Keith Dalgleish	11	40	27.50%	55.93	29.51	29.81	2.25	1.93
Chris Grant	10	80	12.50%	46.00	-3.49	21.45	0.92	0.86
Micky Hammond	10	77	12.99%	46.98	-24.42	18.64	1.05	1.10

KEMPTON PARK

Trainer	Wins	Runs	Strike Rate	% Rivals Beaten	P/L	Run To Form %	Impact Value	Market Value
Nicky Henderson	65	242	26.86%	62.11	-24.31	37.36	2.02	2.19
Paul Nicholls	43	202	21.29%	59.70	-19.27	31.89	1.41	1.64
Alan King	26	180	14.44%	55.05	-81.97	26.10	1.18	1.63
Harry Fry	15	74	20.27%	58.27	-14.88	28.12	1.75	1.85
Philip Hobbs	12	100	12.00%	56.89	-63.53	23.10	0.95	1.52
Chris Gordon	12	70	17.14%	56.17	18.93	24.29	1.49	1.19
Colin Tizzard	12	78	15.38%	56.82	23.10	24.36	1.26	1.13
Nigel Twiston-Davies	12	71	16.90%	52.06	-5.89	19.72	1.44	1.25
Tom George	11	70	15.71%	55.54	-3.00	28.80	1.22	1.24
Dan Skelton	10	133	7.52%	49.89	-99.46	22.78	0.59	1.15

LEICESTER

Trainer	Wins	Runs	Strike Rate	% Rivals Beaten	P/L	Run To Form %	Impact Value	Market Value
Tom George	17	46	36.96%	70.93	27.12	52.23	2.54	1.66
Nigel Twiston-Davies	15	65	23.08%	58.28	23.46	30.78	1.61	1.20
Philip Hobbs	12	27	44.44%	80.09	14.50	55.99	3.05	2.39
Dan Skelton	12	40	30.00%	64.69	12.17	36.08	1.94	1.60
David Pipe	9	29	31.03%	64.59	4.90	48.28	1.86	2.00
Caroline Bailey	9	40	22.50%	55.92	-4.51	30.78	1.48	1.29
Robin Dickin	8	34	23.53%	57.84	22.63	39.35	1.65	1.14
Fergal O'Brien	8	40	20.00%	56.21	26.13	31.39	1.39	1.19
Gary Moore	7	24	29.17%	53.50	1.92	30.56	2.18	1.71
Ian Williams	5	25	20.00%	54.04	-12.18	24.80	1.69	1.59

LINGFIELD PARK

Trainer	Wins	Runs	Strike Rate	% Rivals Beaten	P/L	Run To Form %	Impact Value	Market Value
Gary Moore	12	109	11.01%	49.62	-33.50	20.72	0.83	1.27
Seamus Mullins	11	59	18.64%	51.30	50.88	23.73	1.43	0.88
Nigel Twiston-Davies	8	32	25.00%	61.98	19.58	29.51	1.95	1.58
Warren Greatrex	8	28	28.57%	57.00	-9.66	44.92	2.01	2.25
Chris Gordon	8	45	17.78%	54.18	-15.15	24.98	1.19	1.27
Nicky Henderson	7	15	46.67%	77.01	-1.80	57.14	3.25	3.23
Dan Skelton	6	20	30.00%	71.34	9.75	34.86	2.22	2.09
Lucy Wadham	6	19	31.58%	65.26	41.75	45.44	2.59	1.37
Emma Lavelle	5	19	26.32%	69.45	7.50	38.33	2.32	1.55
Anna Newton-Smith	5	26	19.23%	49.47	8.50	33.33	1.59	1.21

LUDLOW

Trainer	Wins	Runs	Strike Rate	% Rivals Beaten	P/L	Run To Form %	Impact Value	Market Value
Nicky Henderson	31	101	30.69%	65.87	-11.19	42.30	2.47	2.79
Philip Hobbs	29	114	25.44%	65.52	18.87	40.14	2.05	2.14
Dan Skelton	29	129	22.48%	63.93	-14.76	34.26	1.89	2.05
Evan Williams	28	224	12.50%	51.41	-78.69	25.23	0.95	1.21
Tom George	21	112	18.75%	66.34	-17.59	32.70	1.53	1.46
Henry Daly	20	116	17.24%	61.81	-44.12	31.88	1.46	1.44
Kim Bailey	20	107	18.69%	56.99	-14.78	32.55	1.54	1.59
Paul Nicholls	15	59	25.42%	63.00	-14.08	44.14	1.69	2.30
Nigel Twiston-Davies	15	135	11.11%	53.59	-79.09	21.51	0.96	1.48
Venetia Williams	14	113	12.39%	55.81	-39.53	23.17	1.08	1.23

MARKET RASEN

Trainer	Wins	Runs	Strike Rate	% Rivals Beaten	P/L	Run To Form %	Impact Value	Market Value
Dan Skelton	57	209	27.27%	63.99	18.29	36.47	2.02	1.98
Jonjo O'Neill	31	191	16.23%	51.63	-49.14	24.89	1.24	1.40
Brian Ellison	22	145	15.17%	47.87	-37.13	26.04	1.15	1.28
Nicky Henderson	22	73	30.14%	65.66	-2.38	37.67	2.19	2.28
Fergal O'Brien	20	112	17.86%	53.98	3.17	33.84	1.33	1.47
Dr Richard Newland	20	68	29.41%	66.85	25.86	37.28	2.43	2.25
Olly Murphy	18	74	24.32%	64.71	6.38	39.38	1.90	1.67
Peter Bowen	16	84	19.05%	53.18	-8.08	27.66	1.55	1.52
Alan King	15	89	16.85%	58.91	-14.25	30.17	1.28	1.56
Charlie Longsdon	15	122	12.30%	55.34	-63.59	27.25	0.95	1.36

MUSSELBURGH

Trainer	Wins	Runs	Strike Rate	% Rivals Beaten	P/L	Run To Form %	Impact Value	Market Value
Lucinda Russell	33	255	12.94%	50.72	-32.08	24.27	1.00	1.05
Donald McCain	26	135	19.26%	60.47	-8.67	30.98	1.36	1.43
Keith Dalgleish	22	69	31.88%	65.49	12.92	47.76	2.15	1.76
Sandy Thomson	16	74	21.62%	61.21	27.72	31.53	1.64	1.58
Iain Jardine	12	79	15.19%	56.35	4.57	32.47	1.14	1.14
Paul Nicholls	10	26	38.46%	66.50	6.72	50.00	2.37	1.88
James Ewart	9	76	11.84%	50.23	-8.95	23.05	0.98	1.29
Tim Vaughan	9	45	20.00%	56.87	0.08	28.89	1.44	1.35
Rose Dobbin	9	68	13.24%	49.74	-15.25	29.41	1.11	1.20
Jim Goldie	8	85	9.41%	48.63	-29.59	13.32	0.81	0.97

NEWBURY

Trainer	Wins	Runs	Strike Rate	% Rivals Beaten	P/L	Run To Form %	Impact Value	Market Value
Nicky Henderson	42	199	21.11%	60.80	-39.33	34.01	1.97	2.06
Philip Hobbs	26	144	18.06%	57.75	65.76	32.52	1.60	1.56
Paul Nicholls	23	151	15.23%	55.21	-13.18	29.97	1.17	1.55
Alan King	20	174	11.49%	60.61	-79.72	31.01	1.05	1.51
Colin Tizzard	19	110	17.27%	59.81	-10.46	32.66	1.49	1.30
David Pipe	16	93	17.20%	53.21	7.03	28.62	1.64	1.21
Harry Fry	12	72	16.67%	58.35	-20.79	29.12	1.60	2.34
Warren Greatrex	12	76	15.79%	57.00	-14.75	28.43	1.39	1.24
Ben Pauling	12	63	19.05%	51.39	5.36	27.47	1.75	1.35
Dan Skelton	10	91	10.99%	53.58	-36.63	21.85	1.08	1.36

NEWCASTLE

Trainer	Wins	Runs	Strike Rate	% Rivals Beaten	P/L	Run To Form %	Impact Value	Market Value
Sue Smith	19	113	16.81%	60.95	-26.26	29.80	1.32	1.59
Nicky Richards	16	71	22.54%	61.13	-10.61	34.60	1.78	2.13
N. W. Alexander	16	115	13.91%	49.02	-21.55	24.36	1.08	0.99
Lucinda Russell	14	121	11.57%	49.85	-58.47	21.06	0.88	1.15
Brian Ellison	12	55	21.82%	61.55	-16.85	38.74	1.48	1.76
Philip Kirby	10	58	17.24%	54.10	-21.33	27.22	1.26	0.99
Micky Hammond	10	89	11.24%	45.06	-31.63	22.71	0.80	1.00
Sandy Thomson	8	43	18.60%	56.36	-12.47	26.83	1.34	1.48
Keith Dalgleish	8	27	29.63%	59.22	14.00	40.74	2.29	1.66
Nicky Henderson	7	8	87.50%	97.92	5.39	87.50	5.66	3.91

NEWTON ABBOT

Trainer	Wins	Runs	Strike Rate	% Rivals Beaten	P/L	Run To Form %	Impact Value	Market Value
Paul Nicholls	43	149	28.86%	63.86	-45.35	37.02	1.62	2.18
Philip Hobbs	30	143	20.98%	60.93	-22.16	32.49	1.60	1.90
Jeremy Scott	17	93	18.28%	57.33	4.50	22.85	1.55	1.27
Colin Tizzard	17	127	13.39%	57.10	-36.50	23.22	0.97	1.44
Tim Vaughan	15	86	17.44%	52.20	11.79	24.64	1.65	1.27
Evan Williams	14	114	12.28%	53.40	-53.36	20.00	0.86	1.15
David Pipe	13	135	9.63%	48.85	-71.77	16.19	0.81	1.30
Nicky Henderson	13	34	38.24%	65.84	6.65	52.94	2.37	2.20
David Bridgwater	12	46	26.09%	56.74	0.66	35.65	1.83	1.41
Harry Fry	12	51	23.53%	63.16	-5.25	33.99	1.92	1.97

PERTH

Trainer	Wins	Runs	Strike Rate	% Rivals Beaten	P/L	Run To Form %	Impact Value	Market Value
Gordon Elliott, Ireland	79	275	28.73%	67.19	-15.19	43.34	1.93	2.12
Lucinda Russell	29	361	8.03%	47.05	-123.09	18.65	0.60	0.89
Fergal O'Brien	25	90	27.78%	58.94	31.00	34.91	2.00	1.59
Nicky Richards	23	154	14.94%	55.04	-10.54	27.51	1.20	1.39
Donald McCain	23	104	22.12%	52.88	12.43	30.51	1.47	1.31
Lisa Harrison	23	173	13.29%	48.41	-19.58	24.54	1.02	0.89
Nigel Twiston-Davies	18	95	18.95%	54.26	-24.38	23.80	1.39	1.76
Stuart Crawford, Ireland	15	145	10.34%	47.48	-68.19	18.13	0.80	1.01
Peter Bowen	14	36	38.89%	70.60	17.87	50.00	2.75	1.83
David Pipe	12	23	52.17%	79.58	15.61	57.71	2.90	2.04

TRAINERS FOR COURSES

PLUMPTON

Trainer	Wins	Runs	Strike Rate	% Rivals Beaten	P/L	Run To Form %	Impact Value	Market Value
Gary Moore	55	320	17.19%	54.63	-82.27	26.08	1.21	1.54
Chris Gordon	31	175	17.71%	57.23	24.10	32.72	1.34	1.44
Seamus Mullins	16	135	11.85%	48.78	-17.83	17.64	0.83	1.00
Anthony Honeyball	16	59	27.12%	59.35	-8.26	37.48	1.87	1.99
Sheena West	16	90	17.78%	53.37	43.08	25.56	1.42	0.99
Alan King	16	50	32.00%	67.35	-10.28	40.50	2.34	2.65
Neil King	14	72	19.44%	56.89	-18.26	31.52	1.20	1.21
David Pipe	14	56	25.00%	64.46	16.51	32.60	1.83	1.83
Paul Henderson	13	74	17.57%	50.21	-11.12	24.82	1.23	1.00
Colin Tizzard	13	79	16.46%	58.79	-26.42	35.71	1.29	1.25

SANDOWN PARK

Trainer	Wins	Runs	Strike Rate	% Rivals Beaten	P/L	Run To Form %	Impact Value	Market Value
Nicky Henderson	44	161	27.33%	60.38	4.83	37.03	2.26	1.93
Paul Nicholls	25	191	13.09%	54.55	-44.55	27.97	1.00	1.35
Gary Moore	24	142	16.90%	46.49	12.24	23.01	1.24	0.98
Philip Hobbs	16	97	16.49%	58.51	-16.15	26.45	1.47	1.51
Alan King	12	63	19.05%	57.54	6.71	26.98	1.58	1.48
Nigel Twiston-Davies	12	67	17.91%	52.05	42.96	25.37	1.69	1.37
Fergal O'Brien	8	29	27.59%	58.57	23.13	34.48	2.68	1.40
Venetia Williams	8	97	8.25%	50.66	-50.00	20.86	0.70	1.24
Colin Tizzard	8	84	9.52%	47.92	-50.07	17.99	0.83	1.23
Charlie Longsdon	7	65	10.77%	56.04	14.25	19.01	1.09	1.04

SEDGEFIELD

Trainer	Wins	Runs	Strike Rate	% Rivals Beaten	P/L	Run To Form %	Impact Value	Market Value
Donald McCain	50	279	17.92%	56.00	-44.21	29.29	1.21	1.49
Brian Ellison	36	160	22.50%	60.77	-31.78	30.47	1.55	1.58
Micky Hammond	36	276	13.04%	46.06	-88.37	17.40	0.95	0.99
Sue Smith	23	181	12.71%	58.05	-63.62	29.11	0.94	1.43
Neil Mulholland	19	42	45.24%	64.05	19.00	47.62	2.79	2.06
Dianne Sayer	19	93	20.43%	54.73	31.63	25.81	1.70	1.18
Dan Skelton	17	63	26.98%	65.16	-11.03	33.51	1.82	2.22
Joanne Foster	14	84	16.67%	48.58	32.10	28.57	1.17	0.88
Chris Grant	13	154	8.44%	47.21	-42.53	17.84	0.64	0.88
Keith Dalgleish	13	56	23.21%	62.18	-7.47	35.61	1.67	1.75

SOUTHWELL

Trainer	Wins	Runs	Strike Rate	% Rivals Beaten	P/L	Run To Form %	Impact Value	Market Value
Dan Skelton	38	174	21.84%	64.57	-32.42	36.11	1.70	2.10
Jonjo O'Neill	26	168	15.48%	58.79	-40.54	24.80	1.24	1.54
Tom George	22	78	28.21%	68.89	-0.13	44.29	2.05	2.05
Nicky Henderson	18	55	32.73%	69.13	-6.32	40.24	2.16	2.68
Caroline Bailey	17	98	17.35%	57.92	8.75	28.41	1.36	1.35
Charlie Longsdon	13	86	15.12%	53.78	-4.71	21.44	1.21	1.55
Tim Vaughan	13	97	13.40%	53.37	-0.38	23.94	1.08	1.10
Kim Bailey	13	68	19.12%	65.64	-3.16	33.13	1.49	1.73
Alan King	12	45	26.67%	68.37	-12.75	45.49	1.91	1.98
Ben Pauling	12	51	23.53%	61.99	-14.65	38.42	1.99	1.80

STRATFORD-ON-AVON

Trainer	Wins	Runs	Strike Rate	% Rivals Beaten	P/L	Run To Form %	Impact Value	Market Value
Dan Skelton	29	157	18.47%	60.87	-58.49	29.73	1.41	1.91
Warren Greatrex	18	64	28.13%	61.02	12.24	32.58	2.12	2.30
Tom George	17	68	25.00%	61.11	29.57	34.48	1.92	1.79
Philip Hobbs	17	71	23.94%	59.59	25.28	30.44	1.81	1.60
Neil Mulholland	14	79	17.72%	56.51	16.25	23.67	1.35	1.38
Alan King	13	51	25.49%	74.72	-5.81	39.22	2.04	2.07
Peter Bowen	13	61	21.31%	57.67	9.50	33.66	1.69	1.45
Dr Richard Newland	12	41	29.27%	63.95	-13.99	35.97	2.02	2.16
Nigel Twiston-Davies	11	86	12.79%	51.30	-36.47	16.87	1.02	1.41
Donald McCain	11	57	19.30%	58.12	20.88	21.98	1.29	1.11

TAUNTON

Trainer	Wins	Runs	Strike Rate	% Rivals Beaten	P/L	Run To Form %	Impact Value	Market Value
Paul Nicholls	60	194	30.93%	72.63	-14.90	45.13	2.32	2.70
Harry Fry	19	89	21.35%	67.17	-29.56	44.80	1.91	2.31
Colin Tizzard	18	133	13.53%	50.59	-19.85	26.09	1.17	1.36
David Pipe	18	176	10.23%	52.54	-68.42	23.61	0.92	1.29
Philip Hobbs	17	132	12.88%	61.91	-63.98	33.00	1.12	1.82
Jeremy Scott	14	68	20.59%	58.31	40.48	30.25	1.90	1.35
Evan Williams	13	117	11.11%	47.66	-41.83	20.54	0.92	1.06
Nicky Henderson	12	36	33.33%	73.07	3.62	50.00	2.46	2.26
Dan Skelton	11	63	17.46%	51.79	-29.53	32.29	1.48	1.59
Anthony Honeyball	10	56	17.86%	53.29	-11.19	29.04	1.61	1.33

TRAINERS FOR COURSES

TOWCESTER

Trainer	Wins	Runs	Strike Rate	% Rivals Beaten	P/L	Run To Form %	Impact Value	Market Value
Nicky Henderson	16	37	43.24%	81.40	5.32	58.53	3.14	3.05
Kim Bailey	14	57	24.56%	59.81	-2.03	30.43	1.97	1.58
Henry Oliver	11	36	30.56%	64.29	28.50	35.25	2.24	1.52
Ben Pauling	11	50	22.00%	55.66	25.75	32.80	1.85	1.72
Fergal O'Brien	11	44	25.00%	54.96	6.46	33.96	1.95	1.77
Charlie Longsdon	10	52	19.23%	57.30	-17.17	34.70	1.34	1.33
Henry Daly	9	32	28.13%	64.41	25.60	33.37	2.04	1.27
Dan Skelton	9	37	24.32%	62.93	-13.39	36.15	1.84	2.19
Alan King	8	32	25.00%	74.86	-1.80	40.20	2.37	2.90
Martin Keighley	7	52	13.46%	49.37	-18.75	24.06	1.12	1.10

UTTOXETER

Trainer	Wins	Runs	Strike Rate	% Rivals Beaten	P/L	Run To Form %	Impact Value	Market Value
Dan Skelton	68	216	31.48%	66.87	46.86	41.57	2.80	2.24
Jonjo O'Neill	33	254	12.99%	48.90	-82.94	20.23	1.18	1.45
Nigel Twiston-Davies	27	171	15.79%	58.66	-35.01	24.25	1.42	1.56
Charlie Longsdon	25	126	19.84%	57.66	-5.27	28.02	1.78	1.55
Dr Richard Newland	22	73	30.14%	70.64	-5.54	41.14	2.42	2.51
Nicky Henderson	21	75	28.00%	68.00	-22.51	37.00	2.12	2.59
Warren Greatrex	21	77	27.27%	62.67	3.84	40.84	2.25	1.88
David Pipe	20	131	15.27%	55.39	-15.43	25.08	1.41	1.62
Neil King	20	105	19.05%	59.18	-25.51	31.19	1.50	1.44
Philip Hobbs	18	111	16.22%	56.55	-36.96	27.06	1.44	1.71

WARWICK

Trainer	Wins	Runs	Strike Rate	% Rivals Beaten	P/L	Run To Form %	Impact Value	Market Value
Dan Skelton	45	203	22.17%	59.18	-34.81	35.16	1.79	1.91
Alan King	31	146	21.23%	67.18	-54.44	33.89	1.94	2.28
Nicky Henderson	28	86	32.56%	67.68	17.64	42.38	2.73	2.56
Jonjo O'Neill	27	161	16.77%	50.69	60.65	22.91	1.55	1.19
Philip Hobbs	23	109	21.10%	62.85	-9.04	35.66	1.76	2.08
Nigel Twiston-Davies	19	172	11.05%	53.84	-87.31	19.19	0.91	1.31
Paul Nicholls	12	55	21.82%	64.34	-18.79	39.37	1.39	1.77
Venetia Williams	12	85	14.12%	52.72	-29.57	21.44	1.15	1.24
Ben Pauling	12	75	16.00%	49.04	-12.25	21.33	1.69	1.60
Neil Mulholland	12	52	23.08%	53.09	8.42	27.49	1.61	1.21

WETHERBY

Trainer	Wins	Runs	Strike Rate	% Rivals Beaten	P/L	Run To Form %	Impact Value	Market Value
Dan Skelton	37	118	31.36%	67.50	9.50	44.89	2.33	2.13
Philip Kirby	26	157	16.56%	48.96	28.68	25.22	1.51	0.97
Micky Hammond	26	288	9.03%	45.22	-21.92	16.29	0.78	0.80
Sue Smith	21	196	10.71%	53.11	-106.31	22.21	0.85	1.30
Warren Greatrex	19	69	27.54%	62.36	2.68	35.12	2.08	2.35
Jonjo O'Neill	14	65	21.54%	55.50	-7.82	30.98	1.82	1.44
Neil Mulholland	13	39	33.33%	67.68	12.32	38.91	2.84	2.07
Kim Bailey	12	41	29.27%	67.89	17.07	44.20	2.15	2.04
Brian Ellison	12	98	12.24%	56.64	-46.04	22.25	0.94	1.35
Mark Walford	11	79	13.92%	57.02	-10.50	28.37	1.25	1.06

WINCANTON

Trainer	Wins	Runs	Strike Rate	% Rivals Beaten	P/L	Run To Form %	Impact Value	Market Value
Paul Nicholls	99	298	33.22%	66.45	-5.09	43.08	2.29	2.52
Colin Tizzard	36	269	13.38%	55.86	-45.76	24.27	1.10	1.36
Philip Hobbs	21	177	11.86%	55.48	-66.63	23.20	1.03	1.56
Harry Fry	20	100	20.00%	59.35	-14.18	29.11	1.65	1.95
Neil Mulholland	15	153	9.80%	54.19	-39.65	27.83	0.74	1.18
Emma Lavelle	14	69	20.29%	62.61	41.38	28.04	1.81	1.45
Alan King	12	81	14.81%	61.35	-23.11	27.65	1.23	1.80
Jeremy Scott	12	109	11.01%	51.70	-24.13	19.91	0.86	0.93
Venetia Williams	10	72	13.89%	55.30	-27.02	25.32	1.09	1.36
Tom George	10	64	15.63%	58.19	-25.06	26.35	1.18	1.34

WORCESTER

Trainer	Wins	Runs	Strike Rate	% Rivals Beaten	P/L	Run To Form %	Impact Value	Market Value
Jonjo O'Neill	46	266	17.29%	56.68	-54.26	26.22	1.40	1.57
Dan Skelton	34	178	19.10%	58.39	-34.02	28.31	1.53	1.88
Philip Hobbs	34	122	27.87%	63.70	54.47	34.87	2.17	1.80
Neil Mulholland	27	174	15.52%	54.44	-36.80	27.04	1.28	1.34
David Pipe	25	154	16.23%	55.40	-1.89	26.49	1.33	1.40
Dr Richard Newland	25	83	30.12%	69.45	-9.19	42.12	2.22	2.14
Nicky Henderson	25	83	30.12%	67.02	0.93	39.91	2.19	2.33
Peter Bowen	22	105	20.95%	59.82	54.38	30.25	1.75	1.62
Charlie Longsdon	16	104	15.38%	57.63	0.67	24.00	1.28	1.69
Nigel Twiston-Davies	15	91	16.48%	56.14	-10.97	26.43	1.41	1.41

INDEX

Index To Photographers